THE DEATH OF
GEORGE WASHINGTON
HE DIED AS HE LIVED

by

Peter R. Henriques

For

Jeffrey Barlow Henriques, Sr.

July 27, 1908 - November 5, 1995

The Mount Vernon Ladies' Association
P.O. Box 110
Mount Vernon, VA 22191
www.mountvernon.org

Reprinted 2011

This publication was made possible
by the special efforts of

Mrs. C. Lalor Burdick
Vice Regent Emerita for Delaware
and
Mrs. Jared I. Edwards
Vice Regent for Connecticut

and the generosity of the following individuals:

Mrs. Richard Alexander, Vice Regent Emerita for Rhode Island,
and Captain Alexander; Dr. Duffield Ashmead;
Mr. and Mrs. William Atwood; Mr. and Mrs. Daniel P. Brown;
Fenton Brown; Joan Brown; Dr. Robert Cerciello;
Susan Chandler; Mr. and Mrs. Samuel Childs;
Jeffrey Cooley; Mrs. J. Noyes Crary; Patrick Pinnell and Kathleen Curran;
Barbara David; Ethel Davis; Alice M. DeLana;
Jared I. Edwards; Ruth L. Ellison; Mr. and Mrs. James English;
Mr. and Mrs. Thomas Flanders; Dr. and Mrs. John Gibbons;
Shepherd M. Holcombe; Mr. and Mrs. Richard Huber;
The Kohn-Joseloff Foundation; Mr. and Mrs. Sol LeWitt;
Mr. and Mrs. John L. Lowrey; Hugh Macgill and Nancy Rankin;
Michael R. Mahoney; Dr. and Mrs. Robert S. Martin;
Pauline Metcalf; Christopher Monkhouse; Mrs. Stephen D. Paine;
Robert Painter and Nancy Macy; Mr. and Mrs. Millard Pryor;
Mr. and Mrs. David Rhinelander; Mr. and Mrs. Joseph Sargent;
Catharine C. Smith; Mr. and Mrs. Robert H. Smith, Jr.;
J. Peter Spang; Mr. and Mrs. Samuel Stout; Weston Thomas;
Mr. and Mrs. James Tilney; Mutsy Van Vleck;
Judith S. Wawro; and Mrs. Douglas Williams, Vice Regent Emerita
for New York, and Mr. Williams

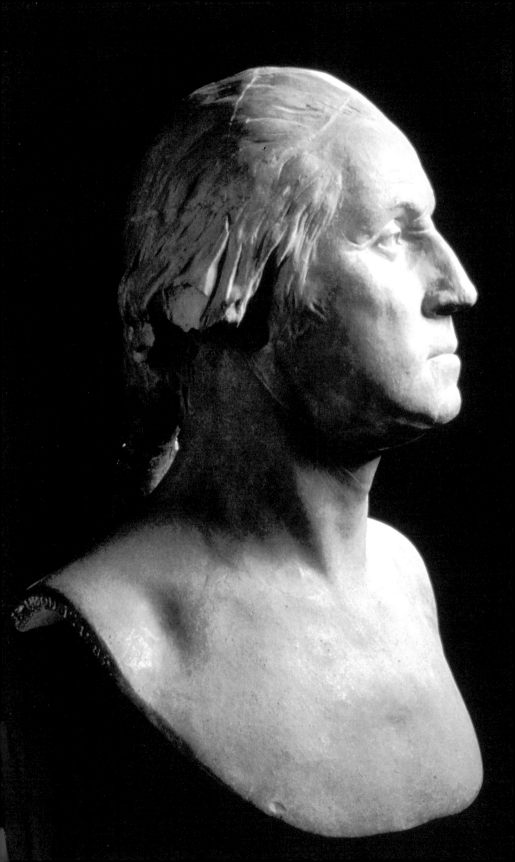

TABLE OF CONTENTS

Foreword vi

Preface viii

George Washington's Final Retirement 1

Washington's Attitude Toward Death 9

Washington's Attitude Toward an Afterlife 19

Washington's Final Illness 27

He Died as He Lived 37

Washington's Death and Funeral 46

Grieving for a Fallen Hero 59

Appendix – Tobias Lear's Journal 66

Endnotes 76

List of Illustrations 86

Death was no stranger to George Washington. Having lost his father Augustine at the age of eleven and his admired elder half-brother Lawrence nine years later, Washington became keenly aware that he "was of a short lived family." As a soldier, Washington first "heard Bulletts whistle" and saw men die from them when he was twenty-two, and the following year he survived the bloody massacre of General Braddock's ill-fated army "although," he remembered long afterward, "death was levelling my companions on every side of me." More deaths followed in the ensuing years on other battlefields and within Washington's domestic circle.

Washington's own death at the age of sixty seven often has been portrayed as a serene passing of a great soul. Two popular prints published soon after he died show a saintly Washington rising through clouds toward a heavenly light. The truth, Peter Henriques tells us in his deeply insightful and engagingly written book, was quite different. Washington died exceedingly hard, and his own views of afterlife were devoid not only of romantic notions, but even of orthodox Christian hope.

With clinical precision, Henriques describes Washington in his last hours as a man struggling desperately for every breath as his well meaning doctors tried to save his life with a prolonged series of futile treatments that only increased his discomfort and introduced an element of indignity to the death room. The purpose of all of these medical details, however, is not simply to be historically correct, but to distill the essence of Washington's character from an honest understanding of the way he died, for this is a book as much about his life as his death.

Although Washington wrote far more voluminously and better than people generally credit, he on most important occasions preferred to let his actions speak for him, and nowhere did they do so more impressively than on his deathbed. Pushed to the extremes of physical and emotional distress for long hours, Washington behaved with remarkable calmness, control, courage, and concern for others, the stoic qualities that defined his inner life of ambition and selfless virtue.

As a youth Washington learned how to satisfy his great hunger for respect and renown by suppressing other appetites, acting disinterestedly and enduring pain when necessary to serve higher causes—Virginia's and Britain's causes during the French and Indian War and America's cause during the Revolution and his presidency. Neither patient or uncomplaining by nature, Washington disciplined himself to persist steadfastly in the face of confusion and adversity, accommodating himself to reality but refusing to abandon essential personal and national goals simply because it became too painful to continue pursuing them.

Washington's ambition, like that which he attributed to Alexander Hamilton in 1798, was "of that laudable kind which prompts a man to excel in whatever he takes in hand." It was his tangible record of meritorious accomplishment, purchased at the cost of considerable exertion and some risk, and the sincerely expressed esteem of his fellow citizens, rather than any divinely promised reward or possible heavenly reunion with loved ones, that sustained Washington at the hour of his death as they had during most of his life.

In this brief but intensively researched and judiciously balanced book, Peter Henriques has succeeded in doing what many writers over the last two centuries have attempted, but only a handful have achieved. He has cut through the tangle of myth that has grown up around Washington to reveal the "real man." In Washington's last hours, Henriques has found the man who not only died as he lived but lived as he died.

— Philander D. Chase
Editor
The Papers of George Washington

PREFACE

Like many people, I have often wondered about death, or more specifically about dying, and how I would react if circumstances allowed me time and the mental capacity to do so. Being at my father's bedside when he died in November of 1995 impressed on my mind the vividness, the emotion, and the power of a deathbed farewell. I discovered that messages could be conveyed and important lessons learned even when communication was difficult.

Knowing that the 200th anniversary of George Washington's death was going to occur in 1999, I decided to take a close new look at Washington's death and see if I could discover more about it and also about his attitude toward death and an afterlife. The result is this little book.

George Washington's final day on earth was to be an excruciatingly painful one as he slowly and torturously choked to death, his suffering magnified by well-meaning but misguided medical treatment. Yet, during the last act of the great drama of his remarkable life, Washington "died as he lived." A close examination of his attitude toward death and an afterlife, and his actions during his final challenge on earth illustrates a great deal about the man and his character.

Since Washington had great difficulty communicating throughout the ordeal, his actions and his words take on added significance. Beyond the intense pain, the disease made speech difficult and often impossible. The circumstances necessarily forced him to be highly selective, but his mind remained clear, and he was fully cognizant of his approaching demise.

Several key parts of his character and personality, which he demonstrated throughout his life, are clearly discernible in his final struggle with death, whom he once personified as "the grim king." The most important are his courage, his sensitivity and concern for others, his desire to be in control, his concern for his personal and historical reputation, his sense of duty, and a philosophy which drew strength more from stoicism than from orthodox Christianity. I have a great many people to thank. The Mount Vernon Ladies Association, under Director Jim Rees, held a symposium at Mount Vernon organized by John Riley, George Washington: Mourning and Memory, in November of 1998. In addition to requesting that I present a paper, George Washington's Final Struggle with the Grim King: Washington's Attitude toward Death and an Afterlife, Jim urged me to expand it so that Mount Vernon could publish it as part of this commemorative series. I owe thanks to many members of the staff of the MVLA for their help in this project—King Laughlin, Michael Moran (a model of efficiency as a publisher), Lisa

Odum, Dennis Pogue, Mary V. Thompson, and particularly the head librarian, Barbara McMillan, who was unfailingly kind and generous with her time and helpful with her suggestions.

Students of Washington are blessed by not only having access to the vast resources of the library at Mount Vernon but also to the Papers of George Washington project housed in the Alderman Library at the University of Virginia. Editor-in-Chief Phil Chase went out of his way to allow me access to various items that have not yet been published and to make me feel welcome in their offices. I also wish to thank members of his staff, Ed Lengel, Christine Patrick, Beverly Runge, and particularly Frank Grizzard for their help, and in Frank's case for especially constructive suggestions and criticisms.

Several friends and colleagues—Don Higginbotham, John Riley, Dorothy Twohig, and Rosemary Zagarri—read over a draft of the book and made helpful suggestions both as to content and form. My son, Dr. Gregg Henriques, shared his wonderful insights into human motivation and helped me better understand the tensions in Washington as he sought fame and glory by the route of self-sacrifice. All of their efforts are most appreciated. Additional help and encouragement came from Sara Bearss, Jack Censer, (my good friend and Department Chair who kept me from retiring early), Larry and Diana Henriques (special cousins and friends), my son Tom Henriques, Mack Holt, Burns Jones, Jack Warren, and my walking partner, Sue Williams, a close friend who let me ruminate on my findings as we logged in our obligatory minutes of exercise.

As a Ph.D. and not a M.D., I needed help understanding the vagaries of diseases such as epiglottitis and conditions like laryngospasm and carbon narcosis. Dr. Anna Guyton, my daughter-in-law, and Dr. Joel LaBow read parts of the manuscript and made helpful suggestions. I want to especially thank Dr. Ken Wallenborn, who coincidentally had removed my son's tonsils over thirty years earlier, for spending several hours with me sharing his vast knowledge and helping me understand what happens both physiologically and psychologically to someone suffering from the malady which afflicted George Washington. Dr. David Morens of the National Institute of Health generously made available his huge collection of articles, many from obscure sources, on various medical conditions connected to Washington's illnesses, as well as his own wide medical knowledge and specific knowledge on the causes of Washington's death. I hope they will feel that I have been medically accurate even if the language is for the non-specialist.

My wife, Dr. Marlene Henriques, and my sister, Judith Pierce, went over the manuscript with a fine-tooth comb and caught many potential errors of grammar or sentence construction. I take full responsibility for those that remain. Beyond thanking her for her specific help with the manuscript, I want to offer special words of appreciation and love to my wife of thirty-nine years whose many achievements have encouraged and inspired me to undertake new challenges. This book would not have been written without her.

Finally, I wish to dedicate this work to the memory of my father, Jeffrey Barlow Henriques, Sr., a remarkable man whose spirit may not live on in the memory of a grateful nation but most assuredly lives on in the memory of a grateful family.

— Peter Henriques

CHAPTER ONE

GEORGE WASHINGTON'S FINAL RETIREMENT

*"I have no wish which aspires beyond the humble and happy
lot of living and dying a private citizen on my farm."*

GEORGE WASHINGTON

March 4, 1797 was a memorable day for George Washington. John
Adams was sworn in as the country's second President. Finally, after
more than twenty years of almost constant and exhausting service to
his country, George Washington was retiring from public life and
returning to his beloved Mount Vernon. "A mind. . . constantly on
the stretch. . . with. . . little relaxation" would at last be employed in
pursuits of his own choosing under his own vine and fig tree.[1] His
joy was scarcely confinable. Adams wrote to his wife the next day,
"He seemed to me to enjoy a triumph over me. Methought I heard
him say, 'Ah! I am fairly out and you fairly in! See which of us will be
the happiest!'"[2]

Joy and relief were not the only emotions which Washington
experienced. After the inauguration Washington went back to his
Philadelphia residence to put some of his papers in order and then
decided to walk to the Francis Hotel to pay his respects to President
Adams. Suddenly behind him the streets were full of people. "An
immense company," one eyewitness called them, "going as one man
in total silence as escort all the way." At the door of the hotel,
Washington turned and looked at them, his cheeks wet with tears.
"No man ever saw him so moved," declared another eyewitness.[3]

Not only was Washington leaving the service of people who
virtually idolized him, he was leaving men he had grown to love,
knowing he might never see them again. He was also leaving the
center stage. Despite his consistent and heart-felt disclaimers, George
Washington was deeply ambitious for fame and glory and drawn to
power as a way of fulfilling deeply held needs. Washington's
attraction to power was not to rule over others but rather to use it to
win the love and admiration of the people he served. Twice before he
had made a final "retirement" from public life, and twice before he
had reentered the spotlight. Only time would tell if a life committed

to glory could find permanent contentment in a life of peace and ease. As he prepared to leave the presidency, Washington was certain the answer was yes. He was ready to make "political pursuits yield to the more rational amusement of cultivating the earth."[4]

While the General's first wish was to quickly return to domestic pleasure, arranging for the shipping of his personal belongings, which besides many individual items filled 97 boxes, 14 trunks, 43 casks, 13 packages and 3 hampers, was a large undertaking. Some of it he would have willing left in Philadelphia. As he confided to his secretary, "on one side I am called upon to remember the Parrot, on the other to remember the dog. For my own part, I should not pine much if both were forgot."[5] Arriving back at Mount Vernon on March 14, the former President found himself extremely busy, although generally happy, trying to bring his beloved Mount Vernon back from years of relative neglect.

He expressed his dilemma in a letter to his friend, the Rev. William Gordon: "An eight years absence from home (excepting short occasional visits) had so deranged my private affairs; had so despoiled my buildings; and in a word, had thrown my domestic concerns into such disorder, as at no period of my life have I been more engaged than in the last six months, to recover and put them into some tolerable train again. Workmen in most countries, I believe, are necessary plagues; in this where entreaties as well as money must be used to obtain their work, and keep them to their duty they baffle all calculation in the accomplishment of any plan, or repairs they are engaged in; and require more attention to, and looking after, than can be well conceived. Numbers of these, of all descriptions, having been employed by me ever since I came home (to render my situation comfortable the ensuing winter) has allowed me little leisure for other occupations."[6]

Despite the problems, GW seemed to be enjoying retirement. The perceptive Henrietta Liston, wife of the British ambassador, noted after visiting Mount Vernon in December of 1797 that the retired hero was "improved by retirement like a Man relieved from a heavy burden. He has thrown off a little that prudence which formerly guarded his every word . . . he converses with more ease and cheerfulness."[7] Unfortunately, GW's joy at once again becoming a "farmer" and a private citizen was not to last. Professor W.W. Abbot explains why: "While it would appear that Washington settled into the rhythm of private life much like any other man, his situation was in fact unique. For one thing, being an icon he attracted an endless stream of visitors, many mere gawkers, whom good manners required he entertain at considerable expense and loss of time. But the thing that complicated Washington's retirement more than anything else was that not only had he been the first President of the United States, he was now also its first ex-President. The ambiguities and uncertainties of the role of ex-President were to lead to his descent for a time from the pedestal on which he had long stood as hero of the Revolution and Father of His Country."[8]

Space limitations prohibit a thorough look at the details of Washington's third and final retirement, but it turned out very differently than GW had hoped. Political partisanship grew ever more intense and greatly worried the master of Mount Vernon who became increasing convinced that the Republican party would risk the safety and well being of the country for their own narrow partisan gains. His estrangement from his former friend, Thomas Jefferson, became complete. He complained to Lafayette that "a party exists in the United States, formed by a Combination of Causes, which oppose the Government in all its measures, and are determined (as all their Conduct evinces) by Clogging its Wheels indirectly to change the nature of it, and to Subvert the Constitution. To effect this no means which have a tendency to accomplish their purposes are left unessayed."[9]

The growing partisanship was intricately connected with what appeared to be an even greater threat to the new nation's security. Revolutionary France virtually declared war on the young republic, seized hundreds of American ships, threatened the lives of American seamen, and treated a peace mission sent by President John Adams with the type of insult and disdain which made war imminent. George Washington found it impossible to simply view these developments as an observer. With his beloved country in danger, Washington responded to the alarm by springing into action. Of course, the country, with war apparently imminent, looked to its greatest hero to once more vindicate her honor and defend her freedom. President Adams offered, with the unanimous support of

Congress, command of all the American forces to Washington, but the evidence indicates that Washington wanted the command and made his availability clear. In Professor Abbot's words, "for all his talk of longing to sit undisturbed under his own vine and fig tree, Washington was not yet quite ready to watch the world pass him by without giving it a nudge or two."[10]

Washington was drawn to power even as he renounced it. Indeed, as Gary Wills has explained, Washington was a master of gaining power by renouncing it.[11] One cannot understand the flesh and blood Washington, as opposed to the mythical Washington, without understanding that Washington's ambition and desire for fame were inextricably interwoven with his ideas of patriotism and service and duty to his beloved country. In retrospect, this final "retirement," like those that preceded it, was more like a recuperative interlude, a chance to restore himself, before inevitably going back into the thick of the battle and the center of the spotlight.[12]

Fortunately, full-scale war did not materialize although Washington's shabby treatment of President Adams and his increasingly virulent partisanship make this one of the less attractive aspects of Washington's remarkable career. For the first time since his campaign for the House of Burgesses forty years earlier, Washington, the absolute champion of non-partisanship, aggressively participated in partisan activities in the Virginia elections in 1799, urging Federalist candidates, including the renowned Patrick Henry, to save the state from control of the Republicans. While he continued to denounce political parties and the new politics was still not to his liking, it was not beyond his understanding, nor beneath his reach.[13] He would do what he could to keep the country unified and safe as he viewed unified and safe, but his strongly Federalist perspective caused some Republican animosity against him.

Despite his continuing concerns and involvement, the threat of war with France receded, and Washington was able to devote more time to his beloved Mount Vernon. A friend left a description of his typical day: "He rides out every morning by day-light, visits all his farms, returns to breakfast, then writes in his library, which is not extensive, answers letters, which are very numerous, dresses and dines at an early hour, between two and three, enjoys a social hour

4

or two, retires sometimes to write or attend to private affairs, takes tea or coffee, and after reading a little, or sitting with friends, he retires to rest at nine o'clock, but eats no supper. He is very active and healthy, cheerful, but moderate in all things."[14]

Discovering some of the animal pens were in bad shape and in need of repair, Washington went out to check on his farms during the day of Thursday, December 12, 1799. Death was not likely to have been on his mind. His recent health had never been better, and he was making various plans for the future. Only days before, he had formulated a meticulous and remarkably detailed plan for the future of his Mount Vernon farms, setting out precisely what should be done over the next three years at every field of every farm, at every meadow, wood, pasture, stable, or pen.[15] The General remained outside for approximately five hours despite the fact that "the weather was very disagreeable, a constant fall of rain, snow and hail with a high wind."[16] Apparently, some time during his travels, Washington was stricken with the virulent infection which would soon claim his life, although it is possible the deadly bacteria were already in his system, waiting for the right conditions to unleash their potency.[17] While the details are vague, there was an epidemic in northern Virginia during the winter of 1799 with the victims exhibiting symptoms roughly similar to those Washington would soon display. Although affecting mainly children, five adults in Alexandria were stricken, and two of them died from the disease.[18]

George Washington's remarkably hardy constitution in this case may have actually worked to his detriment. The day after his death, Thomas Law wrote, "Alas! He relied upon it too much and exposed himself without common caution to the heat in summer and cold in winter."[19] Despite getting wet from the snow and rain, with snow still on his hair and coat, Washington did not change clothes before dinner. Already beginning to show signs of a cold and a sore throat Friday morning, and despite continued bad weather which included sleet, he went out briefly in the afternoon to mark some trees he wished to have cut down. By evening he was very hoarse though still in good spirits. He insisted on reading sections of the newspaper out loud to his wife, Martha, and to his personal secretary, Tobias Lear.

The role of Tobias Lear is central to the story of George

Washington's death. Just as we owe an inestimable debt to James Madison for our knowledge of what happened at the Constitutional Convention in Philadelphia in 1787, so we owe a great debt to Tobias Lear for our knowledge of what happened on the final day of George Washington's life. Both men were motivated by the belief they were participants in a drama of great historical importance and that it was necessary to have a record of it for future generations. [Tobias Lear's account, on which all scholarly accounts are based, is reproduced as an Appendix at the back of this volume, along with an assessment of its strengths and weaknesses as a historical document.]

Lear, a New Englander born in New Hampshire in 1762, educated at Harvard, and a friend of Washington's intimate associate, General Benjamin Lincoln, became George Washington's personal secretary in 1786 and remained so until 1793. While always remaining in close contact and doing various things for Washington and his family, Lear resigned his post to enter what turned out to be an unsuccessful business venture. In 1798 he returned as Washington's full-time personal secretary with the new title of Lt. Colonel after the first president was appointed Lt. General in command of America's forces as war with France loomed on the horizon. Lear would remain with Washington for the rest of the General's life.

Over time, Lear's remarkable competency, reliability, and loyalty won Washington's affection, and Lear became virtually a member of the Washington family. As Washington wrote to the Reverend Joseph Willard, the president of Harvard who had strongly recommended Lear, "His deportment since he came into this family has been such, as to obtain the esteem, confidence, and love of every individual in it." Lear understood this. "In fact, I consider myself as son of the family than in any other light...."[20] When Lear married Mary "Polly" Long in 1790, the Washingtons were so taken with the young couple that they invited them to live with them in the presidential homes both in New York City and Philadelphia. When the Lears had a son, Benjamin Lincoln Lear, President Washington consented to be his godfather. When Polly, only twenty-three, was stricken and died of yellow fever during the epidemic in 1793, President Washington broke a long-standing rule and for the only time during his presidency attended a private funeral. Following

Lear's second marriage to President Washington's favorite niece, Fanny Bassett Washington, the General leased 360 acres of his Mount Vernon estate rent-free to the Lears, a gift Washington would finalize in his will ensuring that Lear and his third wife [Fanny died in 1796] would be able to stay there during the remainder of Lear's life when it would then go to Fanny's children.

Tobias Lear is responsible for much of what is known today about Washington's final hours.

The friendship between Washington and Lear was, at times, sorely tested by incidents that occurred during the long relationship. Lear had moral qualms when Washington took slaves from the new presidential mansion in Philadelphia back home to Mount Vernon to circumvent a new state law that freed slaves living in Pennsylvania for more than six months.[21] Washington, on another occasion, was troubled when Lear used money he held in trust for Washington to satisfy his own personal financial obligations.[22] In such matters, the respect each held for the other saw the friendship through—Washington confident in Lear's intention to repay the money, Lear confident in Washington's intention to eventually free the slaves himself. In the end each man's faith in the other proved justified. Lear himself became quite ill in 1799 and went to the Federal City (Washington, D.C) for several weeks for treatment of "lameness" by Dr. William Thornton. Around this time (May 1), Washington noted in his ledger that he lent his secretary $1,500 in cash, clear evidence of his faith in him as well as affection for him.

The president's affection for Lear was clearly shared by his wife. Martha's fondness for Lear is evident in that following the General's death she presented him with a miniature painting of her husband, along with a lock of his hair and later bequeathed 100 pounds specie to Lear's son, Benjamin Lincoln, in her own will. In turn, Lear described Mrs. Washington as "everything that is benevolent and good."

The evening reading on December 13th was interrupted when Martha left to check on Nelly Custis Lewis, her granddaughter who was confined upstairs following the birth of her first child. Lear then read to Washington on the political situation in Virginia where elections had recently been held. It brought forth some sharp comments from the Federalist General about Republican leaders, James Madison and James Monroe, remarks which Lear, not as staunchly Federalist as Washington, attempted to moderate. As Washington retired to his bedroom, Lear suggested he take medication for his illness. Rejecting the advice, Washington, who seldom took medication, replied, "Let it go as it came."

As George Washington went off to bed he could scarcely have known that it would be his last night alive on this earth. And yet, in many ways, Washington had thought much about his inevitable demise and, while not knowing when it would come, his attitude toward death better prepared him to face the challenge when it appeared.

CHAPTER TWO

WASHINGTON'S ATTITUDE TOWARD DEATH

"The debt of nature . . . must be paid by us all."

GEORGE WASHINGTON

To understand George Washington's attitude toward death, especially during his final retirement (1797-1799), several contrasting points must be kept in tension. Death was in fact often on Washington's mind, but it did not keep him from being extremely active or from planning for the future. His concern about dying was genuine but in no way kept him from focusing on life. Indeed, his philosophy about death and the lack of terror it held for him enhanced the quality of his life. A mixture of fatalism, confidence in a benign Providence, and stoical courage combined to remove the fear of dying for Washington. Yet, while at one level Washington was philosophically reconciled to death and not afraid of it, a careful reading of Washington's correspondence indicates that, at another level, Washington saw death as the end of the life he loved and sought to master. In that sense, death was the enemy.

One oft-repeated theme in Washington's correspondence after he left the presidency in March of 1797 was his expectation that his final retirement would be relatively brief. He was acutely conscious that he was from a "short-lived" family. His father died at age forty-nine and his paternal grandfather at thirty-seven. His half-brothers had both died early and none of his natural siblings lived to sixty-five. In a surprisingly large number of letters following his retirement, Washington made some type of reference to his impending demise. The regularity of the references, with the exception of when he was actively employed as Lieutenant General in 1798, demonstrates that the idea of dying was often on his mind.

Examples abound. He was fast approaching the biblical life span of "three score and ten." His days "cannot be many." "My glass is almost run." His "thread was nearly spun." His life is "hastening to an end." He is "descending the hill"; he is near the "bottom of the hill." He is "approaching the shades below." He has only a "short time" to remain in this "theatre." He is near the end of the "stream

9

of life." He spoke of the "few remaining years of my life," or of a "remnant of a life journeying fast to the mansions of my ancestors." He hoped to spend the remainder of his life "nearly worn" in agriculture "while I am spared (which in the course of things cannot be long)." He speculated about "if I am alive" next year. He refused a wedding invitation because he was "going out of life."

We know that George Washington spent many hours during the summer of 1799 writing a new and very detailed will expressing in clear terms what he wished to have happen upon his demise. According to a letter attributed to his wife, Martha, the decision to write the will was influenced by a very disturbing dream the General had which he interpreted as a sign that his death was imminent. While an interesting vignette, the authenticity of the letter [examined in endnote #23] is highly suspect and should not be used as a window into Washington's thinking. There is another, more plausible, account of Washington touring his plantation with a nephew only days before he died. After pointing out the old family burial vault and the site for the new one, he commented presciently, "First of all, I shall make this change; for after all, I may require it before the rest."[24]

The numerous references to dying should not be interpreted to argue that George Washington was "obsessed" with death or "haunted" by death or that he viewed death in some morbid or depressing fashion. As his major biography observed, "To have avoided all mention of death would have been unrealistic - and Washington was not unrealistic."[25] Indeed, GW was "a rock-ribbed realist."[26] On rare occasions, he could even banter and make light of death. In 1797, the General told his favorite female correspondent, Eliza Powel, of a rather unusual pact he had made. He had "entered into an engagement with Mr. Morris and several other Gentlemen not to quit the theatre of this world before the year 1800." If Washington broke the contract, he trusted he would be forgiven, for he promised to keep his end of the bargain "unless dire necessity should bring it about maugre [i.e. in spite of] all his exertions to the contrary."[27]

More typically, Washington followed the advice of the stoic philosopher, Marcus Aurelius, "It is the duty of a thinking man to be neither superficial, nor impatient, nor yet contemptuous in his attitude towards death, but to await it as one of the operations of Nature which he will have to undergo."[28] In a letter to Landon Carter, in October of 1798, Washington expressed a detached and philosophical view about his health, his increasing age, and his ultimate death. "Having, through life, been blessed with a competent share of it [health], without using preventatives against sickness, and as little medicine as possible when sick; I can have no inducement now to change my practice. Against the effect of time, and age, no remedy has ever yet been discovered; and like the rest of my fellow mortals, I must (if life is prolonged) submit, & be reconciled, to a gradual decline."[29]

George Washington recognized death as an inevitable part of life. It is a debt—a debt to nature—that everyone must pay. "All must die." "There is a time, and a season for all things." There is a time to die and a time to live. Washington clearly viewed the death of his old white servant, Thomas Bishop, as an essentially positive event because of the circumstances. "Altho' [Bishop] should never have wanted victuals or cloaths while he lived, yet his death cannot be cause of regret, even to his daughter; to whom from the imbecility of age, if not when he died, he soon must have become very troublesome to her, and a burthen to all around him."[30] He commented rather casually on the death of two of his own slaves, "the death of Paris is a loss, that of Jupiter the reverse."[31] Death was easier to confront when it was "regular in it's approaches," when one "had lived to an honorable age," and toughest when it "snatched" those from us without warning or struck the young.

While taking death seriously, GW faced it with remarkable equanimity and composure. Stoicism, perhaps acquired from his close relationship with Colonel William Fairfax[32] appears to have influenced his thinking. As the stoic Epictetus expressed it, "Will you realize once and for all that it is not death that is the source of a mean and cowardly spirit but rather the fear of death? Against this fear then I would have you discipline yourself."[33] As far as the record demonstrates, GW was one of those rare men for whom death personally held no terror. By age seventeen, he owned an outline in English of the Principle Dialogues of Seneca the Younger, and the young Washington mastered the advice in one of the chapter heads,

"The contempt of death makes all the Miseries of Life Easy to Us."[34] Seneca also wrote, "He is the brave man . . . that can look death in the face without trouble or surprise." George Washington was one of the valiant men described by William Shakespeare in Julius Caesar: "Cowards die many times before their death; the valiant never taste of death but once."

Washington's stoicism, his fatalistic view that death will come "when it will come," and his lack of fear of its terrors, strengthened by a belief in a benign Providence, empowered him with a composure and courage in the face of danger that was awe-inspiring to his contemporaries. His response to his baptism by fire, "I heard the bullets whistle and believe me, there is something 'charming' in the sound," drew a reaction even from King George II in England.[35] During the French and Indian War, Washington ignored the threats from angry frontiersmen "to blow out my brains,"[36] put his life at extreme risk by going between his soldiers and knocking up their guns with his sword when they accidentally fired at each other,[37] and offered to "die by inches" a horrible death if it would stop the suffering on the frontier he was sworn to protect.[38] He wrote truthfully—if with a touch of arrogance— "I [have]... the resolution to Face what any Man durst."[39]

His legendary courage as commander-in-chief of the Continental Army might have worried his aides but it inspired his men. His actions at Princeton and Monmouth, his response to the falling shells at Yorktown— "cool like a bishop at prayer"[40]—demonstrated a character seemingly immune from normal fear in the presence of death. So great was his courage that even his harshest critics never brought it into question. So extreme was it that one biographer wrote, "There is a streak of something close to a mad nature in a man whose instinctive reaction to near death is sheer exhilaration, who finds the whine of bullets "charming," and to whom the swirl of violence is a fine tonic that calms his nerves remarkably and serves to clear his head."[41]

While part of Washington's courage might have been innate and part a result of his philosophy, some portion of it was inspired by his fascination with the idea of heroic death. Writing at age twenty-seven to Sally Cary Fairfax, Washington mused about the untimely death of a British officer. Rather than mourn the loss, Washington declared, "Who is there that does not rather Envy, than regret a Death that gives birth to honour and Glorious memory."[42] True, the man's life on earth was over, but his reputation and fame would live on. That was something to envy and desire. In the words of one revolutionary orator, "Who, that hath worth and merit, would not quit a present uncertain life to live eternally in the memory of present and future ages?"[43] Cato by Joseph Addison, Washington's favorite play which he often quoted, developed the theme of heroic death. "How beautiful is death, when earn'd by virtue! . . . what pity is it that we can die but once for our country." Several paintings that hung in Mount Vernon's two dining rooms dealt with this theme of heroic death: the death of Richard Montgomery, the Battle of Bunker Hill, the death of James Wolfe, and the death of the earl of Chatham. Some of these paintings dealing with heroic death and military scenes were gifts, but Washington acquired some through purchase.

The General who had faced death so bravely in war had additional opportunities to demonstrate his remarkable equanimity in the face of death after he became President of the new country in 1789. Another pertinent quote from Addison's Cato advises that "your life is not your own when Rome demands it." George Washington lived by that creed. As he wrote his close friend, Lafayette, "But to one who engages in hazardous enterprises for the good of his country, and who is guided by pure and upright views . . . life is but a secondary consideration."[44] Risking your life for your country was a privilege, and if one lost his life in the process, one would have the satisfaction of knowing that in doing so one would win honor and fame. Shortly after his inauguration as president, Washington developed a malignant carbuncle on his thigh which soon threatened his life, and the following year he developed a severe case of pneumonia which caused his physicians and friends to despair for his life.

In both cases, Washington's recorded response was stoical in the extreme. He declared to his aide, David Humphreys, "I know it is very doubtful whether ever I shall arise from this bed and God knows it is perfectly indifferent to me whether I do or not".[45] His physician in the 1789 crisis, Dr. Samuel Bard, recalled Washington's reaction to his illness, "Do not flatter me with vain hopes. I am not afraid to die, and therefore can hear the worst. Whether tonight, or twenty years hence, makes no difference. I know that I am in the hands of a good Providence."[46] During his brush with death in 1790, when all around him were in tears, his wife Martha noted that her husband "seemed less concerned himself as to the result than perhaps almost any other person in the United States."[47] If the burdens of his office seemed to be hastening GW to his grave, it was a price he was willing to pay. "The want of regular exercise, with the cares of office, will, I have no doubt hasten my departure for that country from whence no Traveller returns; but a faithful discharge of whatsoever trust I accept, as it ever has, so it always will be the primary consideration in every transaction of my life be the consequences what they may."[48]

George Washington's calm resignation and willingness to give his life in the course of doing his duty fully comported with his philosophy, but it also tied in with the image he wanted very much to project. For much of Washington's adult life, he was in one sense or another playing a role—the classical republican general, the patriot king, the father of his country.

Washington had a life-long fascination with the theater, and he saw himself as "a figure on the stage" and wanted desperately to play his part well. A heroic death, or at least a courageous death, would be the proper way to exit the stage. Most great leaders are theatrical, and Washington was a master of the correct gesture or action. The image of George Washington as an "actor" is both very useful and also potentially misleading. In Greek, the word "actor" means hypocrite, one pretending to be who he is not. Washington was not an actor in that sense. He believed in and absorbed the role he played. In the words of one biographer, "he was playing the role of George Washington. He was a character actor whose character was himself."[49] Undoubtedly, he was increasingly conscious that everything he did was under close scrutiny and would affect the final result. For complex psychological reasons, Washington desperately wished to have his performance applauded. The desire for the approbation of the people—properly earned through disinterested service for the common good—lay very close to the core of Washington's being.

Washington's equanimity and even occasionally cavalier bravado concerning death should not be misconstrued. GW did not dismiss or downplay the power of and impact of death. Indeed, a careful reading of GW's correspondence indicates that he was never quite able to completely internalize the philosophy he espoused and the philosophy he urged others to accept. To a man who loved life and sought to master and control his environment, death was the enemy who negated and ended that life. No amount of philosophizing ever completely eliminated his visceral reaction to the "grim king."

During his sixty-seven years of life, George Washington often had to face the death of relatives and friends close to him. While there is no extant material for his reaction to the deaths of some people important to him such as his father, Augustine, who died when Washington was only eleven, or his half-brother, Lawrence, who died nine years later at age thirty-four, there still is a significant corpus of material on this subject. Relevant correspondence preserves Washington's reactions to the deaths of such family members as his mother, Mary Ball Washington; his stepchildren Patsy and Jacky Custis; his brothers John Augustine and Charles; his sister Betty Lewis; his nephew George Augustine Washington; his niece Fanny Bassett Washington Lear; and such friends as Burwell Bassett's daughter and Bassett himself; General Nathaniel Greene; Col. Tench Tilghman; Patrick Henry; Henry Lee's first wife and daughter; Benjamin Lincoln's son; Henry Knox's son; William Pearce's daughter; and Archibald Cary's wife.

George Washington's views on the proper way to face death and loss are remarkably consistent throughout his life and include several aspects. At the center was the concept of God or Providence. (Washington uses a remarkable number of different names for this force such as "the Divine Author of the Universe," "the Almighty ruler of the Universe," the "great governor of the Universe," "All-wise Disposer of events," and dozens of others). Washington understood this supernatural force as the giver of life and as actively intervening in human life. The first president has often been described as a deist, but if he was, he best fits into the category of what Edwin Gaustad has called a "warm deist."[50] Deism in the eighteenth century generally denied the interference of the Creator with the laws of the universe, but the image of the great "watchmaker" who created the world but does not intervene in it does not comport with Washington's ideas. In writing to those in time of personal bereavement, Washington consistently stressed three aspects about this supernatural force. It is wise, it is inscrutable, and it is irresistible.

The emphasis was often on the inscrutable nature of Providence. Its actions could not be understood from man's perspective. "The ways of Providence are inscrutable, and mortals must submit." [50A] Man "can only form conjectures agreeable to the small extent of our knowledge and ignorant of the comprehensive schemes intended." It is best to trust Providence "without perplexing ourselves to seek for that which is beyond human ken." [51] Washington recognized that it is often impossible for man to understand why tragedy occurs. And while we may not understand why it occurs, we cannot prevent it from happening. "These are the decrees of an Allwise Providence, against whose dictates the skill, or foresight of man can be of no avail." [51A] Even as a young man he wrote to Sally Cary Fairfax that he had "long believed" that "there is a Destiny, which has Sovereign control of our Actions - not to be resisted by the strongest efforts of Human Nature." [52] He never changed his mind.

Ultimately, Washington fell back on the position that "He that gave has a right to take away." Writing to his dying nephew, George Augustine Washington, he declared, "The will of Heaven is not to be controverted or scrutinized by the children of this world. It therefore becomes the Creatures of it to submit with patience and resignation to the will of the Creator whether it be to prolong, or to shorten the number of our days. To bless them with health, or afflict them with pain." [53] "The alwise disposer of events knows better than we do, what is best for us, or what we deserve." [54] Over and over again, Washington urged those in grief to seek the "comforts of religion and philosophy" but primarily to submit with resignation. Washington reported almost with pride to Bryan Fairfax on how he responded to his nephew's death: "It is a loss I sincerely regret, but as it is the will of Heaven, whose decrees are always wise and just, I submit to it without a murmur." [55]

Yet even as Washington set up an ideal response, he realized the impossibility of actually achieving it in cases of great loss. Instead, he qualified his call for resignation and acceptance with the proviso, "as far as feelings of humanity will allow." Whatever the ideal, he was acutely aware that human beings must grieve for their loved ones. "It is the nature of humanity to mourn for the loss of our friends; and the more we loved them, the more poignant is our grief."[56] Consoling his good friend, Henry Knox, on the loss of his son, Washington recognized that "parental feelings are too much alive in the moment of these misfortunes to admit the consolations of religion or philosophy. . . .Time alone can ameliorate, and soften the pangs we experience at parting."[57]

George Washington certainly grieved intensely for the loss of people close to him, although he did so privately. Adopting the view that controlling sadness was a sign of the triumph of reason over passion and that it was generally unmanly to weep, Washington shunned public displays of grief. Reflecting the mores of the time, Jackie Custis apologized to his step-father for acting "like a woman" upon hearing of his sister's death and giving himself "up entirely to melancholy for several Days."[58] When Custis himself died eight years later following the American victory at Yorktown, an associate noted that General Washington was "uncommonly affected" and stopped writing in his diary in mid-sentence.[59] Washington so regretted General Greene's death that he could "scarce persuade myself to touch upon it."

Absence of specific references to grieving for his father or half-brother, Lawrence, does not mean Washington did not do so. On other occasions, Washington noted that "death of near relatives always produces awful and affecting emotions." "The death of a parent is...awful and affecting." "Separation from our nearest relatives is a heart rending circumstance."[60] Several extant letters further help us understand why we have so few examples of an openly grieving Washington. Writing to Bushrod Washington, son of his favorite brother, John Augustine, who had just died, Washington declared, "To attempt an expression of my sorrow on this occasion would be as feebly described, as it would be unavailing when related." Later, writing Fanny Bassett Washington on the death of her husband, Washington's nephew, Washington asserted, "To express this sorrow with the force I feel it, would answer no other purpose than to revive, in your breast, that poignancy of anguish, which, by this time, I hope is abated."[61] Time and time again

Washington writes that he "feels most sensibly" the loss of a loved one or friend that death has "snatched from us."

George Washington was no marble man. Years after Braddock's defeat he vividly recalled the groans and lamentations of the dying which he said were enough to pierce a heart of stone and certainly pierced his.[61A]

A man of intense passion in many ways, he was passionate—if private—in his grieving for loved ones. Was he consoled by a belief in heaven and the reunion of loved ones after death? Washington's views of an afterlife offer additional insight into his character and why he was able to face his own death in the manner that he did.

CHAPTER THREE

WASHINGTON'S ATTITUDE TOWARD AN AFTERLIFE

"I am about to change the scene."

GEORGE WASHINGTON

Did Washington expect to be reunited with those who were snatched from him by death? George Washington's religious views, including his views on an afterlife, are both complicated and controversial. The strong desire of people to have GW agree with them on these issues makes an objective analysis of his thought difficult. As Richard Brookhiser has noted, "Washington has been a screen on which Americans have projected their religious wishes and aversions."[62] The issue is further complicated by Washington's extreme reticence in discussing matters of religion. If he had a comprehensive philosophy involving the nature of the afterlife, he did not publicly communicate it. The extant evidence is admittedly fragmentary and inconsistent, but a careful reading of what Washington said—and did not say— indicates that while Washington believed in some type of afterlife, his views are only superficially connected to Christianity, and Washington appears to be skeptical about a reunion with loved ones in another life.

The most striking aspect of Washington's view of life after death centers on what he did not say. Not once in all of his authentic, extant correspondence did he explicitly indicate his belief in the reunion of loved ones in Heaven. Certainly the greatest comfort of religion in general and of Christianity in particular is this hope. Washington may have urged those in grief to find consolation in religion, but in all the letters of condolence he wrote he never gave his recipients the comfort of his assurance that he believed they will meet again with their loved ones. In contrast, William Fairfax, following the death of his wife and Lawrence Washington's baby in 1747, wrote to Lawrence, "As it has been the Will of God lately to take to his mercy the spirits of my late Wife and your child we submit to his Divine Pleasure." When George Mason's daughter lost a child in 1785, Mason attempted to console her with the words, "Your dear baby has died innocent and blameless, and has been

19

called away by an all wise and merciful Creator, most probably from a life of misery and misfortune, and most certainly to one of happiness and bliss."[63] Thomas Jefferson comforted John Adams following the death of his beloved Abigail with the thought that Adams should look forward to that "ecstatic meeting with friends we have loved and lost and whom we shall still love and never lose again."[64] Patrick Henry encouraged his sister with the hope "that we shall meet again in Heaven." Washington did not use such language. As Paul Boller writes in another context, there is a "rugged honesty" in Washington's refusal to assume religious postures that he did not feel privately.[65]

Neither did Washington comfort himself with such a vision. Indeed, to the degree that he wrote about death, the emphasis was on separation. "There is something painful in bidding an adieu to those we love, or revere, when we know it is a final one."[65A] After his brother Jack's death, he lamented that he had "just bid an eternal farewell to a much loved Brother who was the intimate companion of my youth and the most affectionate friend of my ripened age." Shortly before his mother died, Washington visited her in Fredericksburg. "I took a final leave of my Mother, never expecting to see her more," he confided to his sister. Parting from his beloved friend, Lafayette, following the end of the war, Washington pined, "I often asked myself, as our Carriages distended, whether that was the last sight, I ever should have of you? And tho' I wished to say no - my fears answered yes."[66] These assertions are not moderated with words as "in this world" or the like.

The argument that George and Martha Washington viewed the concept of an afterlife differently gains support by examining the letters written to each by Jacky Custis on learning of the sudden death of his sister, Patsy, from epileptic seizures in 1773. In his letter to his mother, Jacky urged her to "remember you are a Christian." Patsy's "case is more to be envied than pitied, for if we mortals can distinguish between those who are deserving of grace & those who are not, I am confident she enjoys that Bliss prepar'd only for the good & virtuous, let these considerations, My dear Mother have their due weight with you and comfort yourself with reflecting that she now enjoys in substance what we in this world enjoy in imagination & that there is no real Happiness on this side of the grave." His letter to his stepfather was completely void of such sentiments as if they would not have given solace to Washington.[67]

While George Washington's view of the afterlife does not seem to be a traditional Christian view, careful scrutiny of the extant records makes clear that he did believe in some type of life after death. For example, Washington at least twice made reference to going "to the world of spirits," and also wrote of "the land of spirits." At one point he emphasized the need to get things in order before "I have taken my departure for the land of spirits." He wrote Lafayette about searching for "Elysium," the happy otherworld for heroes favored by the gods. When Patsy died of epilepsy, he believed she had gone "into a more happy, & peaceful abode." Following his mother's death, he reflected the hope that she was in a "happier place." When Tobias Lear's wife died, GW reassured Lear that "she must be happy, because her virtue has a claim to it." Washington hoped that God would bless a group of ministers "here and hereafter." He referred to nurturing the plants of friendship "before they are transplanted to a happier clime."

Apparently, in speaking to the Masons in Philadelphia, Washington made reference to an "eternal temple." In response to a Masonic memorial from Massachusetts, Washington prayed that the members may be blessed and received by the Great Architect of the Universe "in his immortal Temple." To Pennsylvania Masons, GW supplicated "that we may all meet hereafter, in that eternal temple, whose builder is the Great Architect of the Universe."

In a draft written by Timothy Pickering to two Philadelphia churches, Washington looked forward to retirement "which can only be exceeded by the hope of future happiness." While he was dying, he declared several times, "I am going . . . I die hard but am not afraid to go." According to Lear's letter to his mother on December 16th Washington told his secretary, "I am just going to change my scene." Lear wrote Alexander Hamilton that Washington said, "I am about to change the scene." The image of "going" implies some kind of continuation of existing. It is apparent that Washington had difficulty accepting or conceiving of the idea of nothingness. He did not believe that a person simply ceased to exist upon their death.[68]

While life after death goes on, in some fashion, Washington was ambivalent on what type of life it would be. While there are occasional positive references focusing on trusting a benign Providence, Washington more commonly painted a generally gloomy picture of the next world. "The world of spirits" may or may not be a happy place. Washington was "apprehensive" that a colleague whom he had not heard from for many years had gone "to the land of spirits." Clearly, GW was indicating he thought his correspondent was dead, but the implicit point of the quote was that it was better to be alive on this earth than to have gone to the "land of spirits."[69]

When Washington spoke of Patsy going to a happier place, he specifically contrasted it with "the afflicted Path she hitherto has trod." A relative had written Washington that his Mother was in fact in a happier place. Washington significantly added his hope that this was true rather than simply agreeing with the statement.[70] The passing reference to Elysium may well have been made tongue in cheek (as for example when Washington refers to looking into the 'Doomsday Book'). Washington occasionally wrote of Heaven as a place, but generally he used Heaven as a synonym for Providence or God. While there are clear references to an afterlife and some of them are quite positive, Washington's references to death and what follows are more often rather gloomy and pessimistic.

Rather than viewing death as the gateway to a better world, Washington often described death with emotive words such as a "stroke," "a severe stroke," a "blow," a "trial," a "test," "an afflictive trial,", a "debt" we must all pay. One pays "the final debt." The retiring president looked forward to rural pleasures "while I am spared." It is again worth noting the negative way Washington phrased it. One hoped to be "spared" to enjoy this world rather than looking forward to be "called" to a better world. Death was "the grim king" whom Washington, not yet thirty and very near his "last gasp," feared would master his "utmost efforts" and cause him to "sink in spite of a noble struggle."[71] A gravely ill friend had "in a manner shaken hands with death."[72] To demonstrate how much he did not want to take on yet another new responsibility, Washington told Alexander Hamilton that he would leave his peaceful abode with as much reluctance as he would go to the tomb of his ancestors.[73] If he died before 1800, it would be despite his best efforts to keep himself alive. When people died, GW spoke of them as "poor Patcy" or

"poor Greene" or "poor Laurens" or "poor Mr. Custis" or "poor Colo. Harrison." He talked about his own "approaching decay," of death as going "to the shades of darkness," "to sleep with my fathers," "to the shades below," to "the country from whence no Traveller returns," "to the tomb of my ancestors," to the "abyss, from whence no traveller is permitted to return," "to the dreary mansions of my fathers."[74] Taken together, the overall image projected is not a bright one, certainly not a traditionally Christian one.

The Christian images of judgment, redemption through the sacrifice of Christ, and eternal life for the faithful find no resonance in any of Washington's known writings. The main reason for this is because, as Barry Schwartz noted, GW's "practice of Christianity was limited and superficial."[75] George Washington can accurately be called a Christian but only by defining the word in very broad terms. Many would argue that it is difficult to be a genuine Christian without a belief in Christ and in the redemptive power of Christ's love and his sacrifice in order to ensure the forgiveness of sins and the hope of life everlasting.

The total and complete lack of the use of the words, Jesus Christ, or terms like saviour or redeemer in George Washington's personal correspondence is a remarkable fact. The absence is so total that it is logical to conclude that it was a conscious decision by Washington for one reason or another. He does not even refer to Jesus as a great moral teacher or prophet. There is simply no reference to the person, Jesus, either implicit or explicit, almost as if GW had made a taboo of the words, Jesus Christ. (There are a few references in his public papers, most notably in his Circular Letter to the States in 1783 which refers "to the divine author of our blessed religion."[76] Interestingly, even in these few instances they are never in GW's handwriting).

In a revealing letter to Lafayette, to whom he wrote with a frankness shared with few if any other correspondents, Washington described Christianity as if he were an outsider. "Being no bigot myself to any mode of worship, I am disposed to endulge professors of Christianity...that road to heaven, which to them shall seem the most direct plainest easiest and least liable to exception." Douglas Freeman wrote that at age twenty-seven Washington found "no rock of refuge in religion." Forty years later, he still had not found it.[77]

The word George Washington used most consistently in describing Providence or God was "inscrutable." If Providence is in fact inscrutable, then it is not possible to receive any revealed truth about its way through ministers, priests, prophets, or messiahs. Neither could religious ceremonies and sacraments influence the situation.[78] Since GW does not see the truth revealed so that there can be no legitimate dispute as to what it is, all that remains is to act in concert with your conscience which has more power for GW than revealed religion. The final rule from the "Rules of Civility", which GW copied as a youngster and which influenced his adult life, was to "keep the heavenly spark of conscience alive in you." This he did. "While doing what my conscience informed me was right, as it respected my God, my country and myself, I could despise all the party clamor and unjust censures which might be expected from some."[79] GW was confident he knew what was "just" and "right," and he did not need to rely on revealed religion or a Holy Book to tell him so.

Perhaps the best way to view GW is to realize that he "was a man of honor, not a man of religion." His ethics are more Stoic than Christian. "The one [Christian] considers vice as offensive to the Divine being, the other as something beneath him."[80] In Freeman's words, "GW was just because justice was right and because lack of it would cost him some of his self-respect. He could not be fair to himself if he were unjust to others."[81]

Washington appeared to be more interested in acquiring a different type of immortality than that offered by Christianity. He sought a secular immortality by achieving fame across the ages. In another interesting letter to Lafayette, Washington discussed the "bards," those poets "who hold the keys of the gate by which Patriots, sages and heroes are admitted to immortality!" The ancient bards are called "both the priests and the door-keepers to the temple of fame." David Humphreys understood the General's desires when he wrote him in connection with the Houdon bust, "Indeed, my dear General, it must be pleasing to you amid the tranquil walks of private life to find that history, poetry, painting and sculpture will vie with each other in consigning your name to immortality."[82] One can sense the heartfelt agreement that Washington shared when he wrote to the father of his wartime aide, Tench Tilghman, "there is this consolation to be drawn, that while living, no man could be more esteemed - and since dead, none more lamented than Colo. Tilghman."[83]

To be revered in life, to be lamented in death, to be remembered with honor in history were things that could give real consolation in a time of grief and smooth the bed of death. George Washington had striven, with remarkable success although at a fearful price, to win the praise of right-thinking people, to seek fame but without making "improper compliances for what is called popularity."[84] George Washington had passed every test. Only the final test, paying the final debt of human nature, remained.

CHAPTER FOUR

WASHINGTON'S FINAL ILLNESS

"I die hard."

GEORGE WASHINGTON

When his sole surviving brother, Charles, died earlier in 1799 Washington wrote, "I was the first, and am now the last, of my fathers children by the second marriage who remain. When I shall be called upon to follow them, is known only to the giver of life. When the summons comes I shall endeavour to obey it with good grace."[85] He hoped that in facing death he would do nothing to sully the reputation he had spent a lifetime building. Of course, Washington could not know when the final test would come, but he hoped and expected that he would meet the final summons "with good grace." He could not have imagined just how difficult the final challenge was going to be.

Although George Washington went to bed willing to let the disease "go as it came," the situation rapidly deteriorated. By the early hours of Saturday morning, the 14th, the disease had progressed so rapidly that Washington, feverish, awoke very uncomfortable and with labored breathing. Alarmed, Martha wanted to seek help, but Washington, concerned that going out into the cold night air might lead to a relapse (Martha had only recently recovered from a serious illness), did not permit her to do so. Martha's acquiescence to her husband's request, despite her deep concern for his well being, sheds light on their relationship. Except in the area of her children and grandchildren, George Washington made the major decisions and Martha supported him in those decisions. Martha Washington's role in George Washington's life was absolutely crucial. Not only did her wealth allow him to enter into the very first rank of Virginia planters and enjoy the independence that went with great wealth; even more importantly, she gave him a much needed psychic security and was an indispensable support as he bore the increasingly heavy load of fame and responsibility. Twice in his final will, Washington, who chose his words carefully, referred to Martha not only as my "wife" or my "beloved wife" but as my "dearly beloved wife." He described her as "the partner of all my Domestic enjoyments," and made ample provision for her in the will. While their union might have lacked some of the fire of a Hollywood romance (Mrs. Liston described GW as "more a respectful than tender husband"), it was a very strong and mutually satisfying relationship.[85A]

The comments about Martha from those visiting Mount Vernon are almost universally complimentary. In William Thornton's words, Martha was a "very agreeable, lively, sensible person, and has the remains of great beauty."[86] To another, she was "a plain good woman very much resembling the character of Lady Bountiful, is very cheerfull & seems most happy when contributing towards the happiness of others."[87] A third described her as "the very essence of kindness. Her soul seems to overflow with it like the most abundant fountain & her happiness is in exact proportion to the number of objects upon which she can dispense her benefits."[88] She was "the amiable partner of his toils and dangers, who shared with him the anxieties of public life and sweetened the shades of retirement."[89]

Martha "almost adored" her husband and in the words of one eulogist, her life-long smile smoothed the hero's brow.[90] Her main mission in life was to support her husband, to be his confidante, and to defer to him on such matters whether it be on major alterations to Mount Vernon, when she should visit him in camp, or what she should include in her letters which he often wrote and she simply copied. Thus, even in the face of a grave illness, Martha yielded to her husband. For approximately four long hours, they waited together, Washington laboring for breath, Martha sick with worry, until Caroline, one of the household slaves, finally arrived some time around 7 a.m. to light the fire in their room, and Martha could at last send her to summon Colonel Lear and help.

Lear dispatched a servant posthaste to alert Dr. James Craik in Alexandria of the crisis. Meanwhile, Washington, himself a firm believer in blood-letting, ordered that George Rawlins, his overseer on Union Farm, come to Mount Vernon to bleed him. Martha, worried that the process would be harmful, tried to stop it, but once more Washington asserted himself and commanded, as soon as he was able, "More." It would be the first of four bloodletting sessions in the next ten hours. Then Lear applied "sal volatile," the menthol-vapor rub of the time, to GW's throat, wrapped a piece of flannel saturated with the same evil-smelling salve around his neck, and bathed his feet in warm water, all without noticeable effect.[91] Shortly after 9 a.m.,[92] Dr. Craik alighted from his horse in front of the mansion.

Dr. James Craik hurried to George Washington's side, not simply as his physician but as his oldest and most intimate friend. Craik, born in Scotland around 1730 and educated at Edinburgh to be a physician in the British army, came to America around 1750. While the surgeon for the Virginia regiment during the French and Indian War, he and Washington began their lifelong friendship. No one, save Martha herself, was closer to Washington than his "compatriot in arms, and old and intimate friend," words Washington used to describe Craik in his will. As a token of esteem, GW left him "my Bureau (or as the cabinet makers call it, Tambur Secretary) and the circular chair, an appendage of my study."[93]

The indications of their special closeness are numerous and revealing. (There would undoubtedly be more examples except that the personal letters between the two, which Craik preserved, were later unfortunately either lost or destroyed.) One surviving letter indicates Craik could write the president in a bantering fashion: "She [his daughter, Nancy] begins to be tierd of her fathers house and I believe intends taking an old Batchelor Mr. Hn [Robert Harrison] as a play mate Shortly."[94] Craik named one of his sons, George Washington Craik, to honor his friend. Washington in turn helped pay for the boy's education and later, as president, offered him a post as his personal secretary. When GW became president, he had his two nephews, George Steptoe and Lawrence Augustine Washington, move into Dr. Craik's home and under his care while they attended school in Alexandria. Craik, at Washington's urging, had moved there in 1784 from Port Tobacco, Maryland. Twice, as virtually Washington's sole companion, Craik went on trips with his old commander to examine GW's western lands. He was frequently called to Mount Vernon to minister to ill slaves. When Washington thwarted a plot by some of his slaves to escape from Mount Vernon [touched on below] he used his friend as a trusted intermediary.

Probably no one who was not a family member spent more time at Mount Vernon. When David Humphries wrote the family from Europe the one non-family member he wished to be remembered to was Dr. Craik. Described as an "intimate" of Nelly Custis Lewis, Craik attended her when she gave birth to her first child in November of 1799. Martha thought so highly of him as a friend and physician that she would not allow him to leave her during the more than two weeks of her own final illness a few years later.

Washington had great respect for Craik as a physician as well as a friend. During the American Revolution, Washington offered Craik his choice of two important medical posts, but added the proviso, "I have no other end in view than to serve you; consequently, if you are not benefitted by the appointment, my end is not served."[95] Craik accepted GW's offer to become deputy director general of the hospitals in the middle department. He served throughout the war, becoming one of the three chief hospital surgeons in October 1780 and chief physician and surgeon of the army in March 1781.[96] During the war, Craik warned his old friend of the Conway Cabal, dressed Lafayette's wound at the Battle of Brandywine, and was at Jacky Custis's deathbed after Yorktown.

Nowhere did Washington make his confidence in Craik clearer than in a letter to his assistant Secretary of War, James McHenry, in 1789: "The habits of intimacy and friendship, in which I have long lived with Dr. Craik, and the opinion I have of his professional knowledge, would most certainly point him out as the man of my choice in all cases of sickness. I am convinced of his sincere attachment to me, and I should with cheerfulness trust my life in his hands."[97] When he was stricken with a malignant tumor early in his first term, Washington expressed confidence in his physicians but wished Craik could also examine him. He wrote his friend, "I confess I often wished for your inspection of it."[98] When Washington accepted command of the American armies in 1798 to meet the threat of war with France, his first appointment was to make his old friend the Surgeon General of the army. Supporting his decision, Washington opined, "If I should ever have occasion for a physician or surgeon, I should prefer my old surgeon, Dr. Craik, who from 40 yrs. experience, is better qualified than a dozen of them together."[99]

Craik's forty years of experience helped him to realize that his dear friend's illness was likely terminal. Martha Washington, following Craik's standing advice on what to do in an emergency, had already asked Tobias Lear to send word to Dr. Gustavus Brown in Port Tobacco to come to Mount Vernon as quickly as possible. Brown was a wealthy Edinburgh-trained physician and horticulturist. The star of a prominent medical family, Brown was both a "renaissance man" and a physician respected for his bedside manner. In 1799 he had been busy co-founding the Medical and Chirurgical [Surgical] faculty of Maryland. Lear scribbled, "Mrs. Washington's anxiety is great, and she requests me to write you desiring you will come over without delay, as it is impossible for the General to continue long without relief."[100] Fearful that Brown might not arrive in time, Dr. Craik quickly decided to send word to his fellow physician and Mason, Dr. Elisha Cullen Dick, of Alexandria. Craik understandably did not want to face the responsibility of caring for America's greatest hero all by himself and welcomed the help of the younger but very highly regarded Dr. Dick, a graduate of the University of Pennsylvania and a student of the renowned Dr. Benjamin Rush.

Over the years there has been considerable debate on the nature of Washington's final illness with "quinsy" being the usually stated cause although Drs. Dick and Craik officially declared that Washington died of "cynanche trachealis," a term for an inflammation of the upper windpipe and often used to describe croup. It is of course impossible at this late date to assert with certainty what malady struck the General, but the latest and most convincing medical studies indicate that George Washington died from acute epiglottitis caused by a virulent bacteria, possible Hemophilus influenza type b. or some type of streptococcal bacteria. The epiglottis is a cartilaginous structure located at the base of the tongue and at the entrance to the larynx (voice box). It is positioned high in the throat at the very entrance to the airway which goes through the larynx to the trachea, commonly called the windpipe, and then into the lungs. During swallowing, the epiglottis rises and its lateral folds close over the entrance to the larynx, preventing food and drink from being inhaled. When the epiglottis swells, the airway is at risk of obstruction (in acute cases, the epiglottis may swell to greater than ten times its normal size). The swollen epiglottis may partially obstruct the airway, and in severe cases a ball-valve-like effect can nearly completely obstruct airflow causing a whistling noise called stridor. Washington exhibited many symptoms consistent with classic acute epiglottitis. These included: rapid onset, high fever, an extremely sore throat, great difficulty in swallowing, drooling, great difficulty in speaking without true hoarseness, increased airway obstruction, especially when leaning backward, a desire to assume a sitting position in spite of weakness, persistent restlessness, and finally an apparent improvement shortly before death. It is a "textbook" case of this extremely painful and frightening disease.[101]

Accounts of George Washington's death uniformly downplay the horrific nature of the illness and the amount of suffering he had to endure. While recognizing that he "suffered intensely," Tobias Lear, in his effort to portray Washington's death as heroic, contributed to this assessment of a peaceful end to his life. Lear's words, "he died without a groan or a sigh," were quickly seized upon by the myriad of Washington's admirers who did not want to picture him suffering. In the words of one of those admirers, "It is a pleasing consideration to all who loved him that he went off with so little pain."[102] The view that Washington experienced a peaceful and "beautiful death" was soon widely held. Parson Weems, Washington's first biographer and the man responsible for many commonly held myths about him, informed his readers of GW's actions as he felt that his spirit was ready to leave his body. Washington "closes his eyes for the last time, with his own hands - folds his arms decently on his breast, then breathing out 'Father of mercies! take me to thyself' he fell asleep."[103] The headline of a story in the *Alexandria Gazette* in 1931 proclaimed, "The Beautiful Death of the Great Washington, Met End Serenely, Surrounded by Loved Ones."[103A] Such views are widely held today. In a recent article celebrating the bicentennial of Washington's death, a prolific student of Washington writes, "It is hard to find anywhere else in history... a more serene death scene."[104] The truth is very different.

Bryan Fairfax, one of Washington's closest friends and his last dinner guest at Mount Vernon, understood the import of Washington's confession, "I die hard." Fairfax noted this was "a great thing from him, because he was one of the last Men to complain.

One Expression of that sort from him, to me shews more Suffering than 100 Groans from almost any other Man."[105] Washington's willingness to face "what any Man durst" had been demonstrated time and time again. Washington fit the image of the stoical man described by ancient philosopher, Seneca, as one "who, if his body were to be broken upon the wheel or melted lead poured down his throat, would be less concerned for the pain itself than for the dignity of bearing it."[106]

The pain associated with acute epiglottitis is intense. The inflamed swollen epiglottis, bright red and about the size of a plum, is similar to a raw sore in a very sensitive spot and is extremely painful. As the stoical Washington described his throat to Lear, "tis very sore." The physical pain, severe as it might have been, was not the worst part of his illness. The truly frightening aspect of acute epiglottitis is the obstruction of the larynx which makes both breathing and swallowing extremely difficult. The first thing an infant learns to do is breathe and the second is to swallow. To have these two absolutely basic functions dramatically impaired is very frightening to anyone, no matter how brave and courageous he or she might be. Like any mortal, George Washington had to face the terror of air hunger, of smothering and gasping for each breath, and his constant restlessness and changing of positions throughout the day were part of his endless effort to meet this most basic of needs.

There was not one thing done either for or to George Washington during his illness which was not done out of love and with the very best of intentions. Yet, tragically, virtually every single action in fact compounded his suffering and hastened his demise. Even simple ministrations almost proved fatal. Lear recounted, "A mixture of Molasses, Vinegar & butter was prepared to try its effects in the throat; but he could not swallow a drop. Whenever he attempted it he appeared to be distressed, convulsed and almost suffocated." The fluid was forcibly and convulsively rejected. This reaction was caused by the swollen epiglottis which blocked the mixture from going into the esophagus and caused some to go into the windpipe, triggering a laryngospasm. When food or water goes "down the wrong pipe," one chokes and coughs because the larynx immediately goes into a sustained spasmodic closure to prevent inhalation of foreign substances into the lungs. During this

Blood-letting instruments, common tools in 18th-century medicine, were used to draw approximately five pints of blood from Washington in less than 12 hours.

laryngospasm, air can neither enter nor exit the lungs. This is uncomfortable under normal circumstances, but it can be fatal when the airway is already partially compromised and breathing and swallowing are impaired.

Following Washington's death, Dr. Brown wrote rather incautiously to Dr. Craik and frankly worried that perhaps their treatment had hastened or even caused the death of their famous patient, but he added, "we were governed by the best light we had; we thought we were right; and so we are justified."[107] There is much truth in this observation, and charges that his physicians virtually murdered him are certainly unfair. According to the accepted medical practice of the time, Washington received excellent care from the three attending physicians. The regime proposed by Dr. William Cullen, well known Professor of Medicine at Edinburgh, was followed almost exactly. Nevertheless, it is true, that however well

34

intentioned and sanctioned by the experts of their day, most of their treatment was in fact detrimental and significantly added to Washington's discomfort. Sadly, there was still truth in the lines of Moliere's play, Le Malade Imaginaire, written in 1673: "Nearly all men die of their remedies and not of their illnesses."[108] The main weapons in the physician's arsenal were unchanged: bloodletting, purgatives, emetics, enemas, and blistering, and they were often ineffective and harmful.

During the course of less than twelve hours, George Washington was bled four different times, losing approximately five pints or over eighty ounces of blood! This was between one third and one half his blood volume. Medical practitioners believed that diseases were caused by an imbalance between the overabundance of the four humors within the human body: blood, phlegm, black bile (melancholy), and yellow bile (choler). The course of treatment encouraged evacuation by bloodletting, vomiting, or purges.[109] Of course, the theory behind phlebotomy was to remove the diseased matter from the body, and practitioners incorrectly assumed that the blood would be restored within hours. They also hoped the bloodletting would reduce the swelling around the infected area, and in this case it might have had some effect, as GW was able to swallow a bit more easily later in the day. Nevertheless, the fact is such excessive bloodletting severely weakened Washington. In addition, the aggressive treatment compromised his circulation. In acute epiglottitis, it is not as difficult to exhale as to inhale and receive sufficient oxygen. As a result, the patient suffers from hypoxia, deficient oxygenation of the blood. The very significant loss of blood further reduced his oxygen carrying capacity as the hemoglobin in the blood carries the oxygen. The use of purgatives significantly reduced his bodily fluids and exacerbated the situation by further compromising his circulation.

Not only did the purgatives compromise circulation, they inflicted significant additional suffering. Repeated doses of emetic tartar totaling five or six grains were given to induce vomiting. Two moderate doses of calomel (a white tasteless medicine with mercurial properties used as a purgative) were given, an injection was administered, followed by ten more grains of calomel. The result was a "copious discharge of the bowels." How much discomfort this would cause a man who was struggling for each and every breath is easier to imagine than to describe. While not mentioned by Lear, the room must have reeked of "blood and stench and sweat."[110] A blister of cantharides was applied to the patient's neck. Cantharides are dried Spanish fly ground into a powder and applied to the skin to cause blistering. While it added to his discomfort it did nothing to alleviate the situation. In view of the virtual torture that he was enduring, it is not surprising that Washington, who appeared to realize relatively early on that the disease would prove fatal, struggled valiantly to convince his physicians to stop their ministrations. He pleaded, "Let me go off quietly."[111]

The extreme difficulty in speaking and making his wishes known added to Washington's agony. Drs. Dick and Craik reported, "Speaking which was painful from the beginning, now became almost impracticable." Tobias Lear later informed Alexander Hamilton, "He could only speak at intervals and with great difficulty," and this prohibited him from saying many things that he wished to communicate.[112] Although speaking was very difficult, it was not impossible, and George Washington's communication that fateful day, both by word and action, reveal a great deal about the man and his character. Confronting a terribly frightening and painful disease, facing an unceasing effort to obtain sufficient oxygen, fully cognizant he was dying, George Washington somehow managed through a remarkable display of will power and self-control to summon up the strength to communicate his most pressing thoughts and wishes to those around him. During his long and distinguished life, Washington had many "finest hours." Here in his sick room, despite the presence of "sweat, stench and blood" and impending death, George Washington once again rose to the occasion and confirmed his greatness.

CHAPTER FIVE

HE DIED AS HE LIVED

*"When the summons comes I shall endeavour
to obey it with good grace."*

GEORGE WASHINGTON

One of Washington's most endearing traits is that he combined a sense of power with diffidence. George Washington was a remarkable man, knew he was a remarkable man, and was revered by the American people as an almost god-like figure. He was feted, praised, honored, and almost worshipped in a way no other American ever has been. Nevertheless, in spite of this "specialness," Washington never lost sight of the shared sense of humanity. In Robert Frost's words, "George Washington was one of the few in the whole history of the world who was not carried away by power."[113] Abigail Adams observed that all the praise and adulation "never made him forget that he was a Man, subject to the weakness and frailty attached to human Nature."[114] In William Thornton's words, Washington always remembered that in a fundamental way, "man is equal to man."[115] GW's diffidence and shyness allowed him to keep a healthy psyche and not let the constant adulation go to his head. He never saw himself as intrinsically superior to others, and this basic respect and concern for others, combined with his charisma and power, were two of the keys to his success as a leader.

Two small vignettes from his retirement years, and they could be multiplied many times over from throughout his life, illustrate this aspect of Washington's character. The British actor, John Bernard, recounted how he had happened upon an overturned carriage moments after George Washington (whom Bernard did not immediately recognize) had rushed to help a female passenger laying unconscious by the roadside. Bernard then "described what followed as the hale, well-made man, still vigorous although evidently advanced in years, strained to free a carriage buried under half a ton of luggage."[116] Most country gentlemen would have had their servants render aid, but Washington did it himself. An avid theatergoer who had seen Bernard perform, GW recognized Bernard and invited him to Mount Vernon. Bernard recorded the experiences of the day and went away deeply impressed with the character of the remarkable man he had just met.

Elkanah Watson visited Mount Vernon in 1785 and recounted how Washington put him at ease "by unbending in a free & affable conversation." During the night, Watson suffered from a terrible cough. Suddenly, there was the General himself, having gotten out of bed in the middle of the night and now standing at Watson's door with a bowl of hot tea and the desire to be of service. In Watson's words, "As a trait of the benevolence & private virtue of Washington, it deserves to be recorded." [117]

This concern for and sensitivity to others was not a thin veneer, an act put on either to please or to deceive people. It was an essential part of Washington's persona, so integral to his character that even in the midst of a mortal and very painful illness he demonstrated it a number of different times. His concern for Martha's welfare, even at the potential cost of his own, was recounted previously in this book. When his overseer, George Rawlins, summoned to bleed the General, manifested nervousness and anxiety about performing such an operation on his illustrious employer, GW reassured him, "Don't be afraid."

In the course of the long and agonizing day, Washington consistently apologized to those trying to care for him and ease his suffering for the trouble he was causing them. Such actions speak volumes about Washington's character. He apologized to Tobias Lear who was helping move him to different positions in his endless hunger for air by worrying that the effort would fatigue Lear! "I am afraid I shall fatigue you too much." Lear further noted that when speaking was too difficult, Washington "looked at me with strong expressions of gratitude." He thanked his physicians for their heroic efforts and never complained about the pain they inflicted upon him. He even urged his personal body servant, Christopher Sheels, who was standing by the bed throughout the day, to sit down. How many powerful leaders, in the midst of an excruciating terminal illness, would either notice or be concerned with the fact that a personal servant had been standing on his feet for most of the day. It was the last request GW personally made of his body servant, and it was one that Christopher was probably happy to oblige. We do know that he sat down, but sadly, unlike the other three people immediately around his deathbed, we have no idea of what Christopher was thinking as he watched his master's final struggle.

Symbolically, it was fitting and proper that Christopher, as well as other household slaves (Charlotte, Caroline, Molly), be present at the end of Washington's life for slavery played a key role throughout his life and career. Limited as the information is, the extant record on the relationship between Christopher and Washington indicates just how complex and convoluted the issue of slavery was. At the time of Washington's death, Christopher was still a young man, born in 1775 or 1776, son of Alce [Alice], a spinner, and the grandson of Doll, the first cook for Mount Vernon. In time, Christopher replaced the comparatively famous William "Billy" Lee, as GW's personal body servant. "Billy" had ridden by the General's side throughout the entire war for independence, but by the 1790's two crippling injuries made it impossible for him to effectively continue in Washington's service. Two very different surviving vignettes indicate the complicated relationship between Washington and Christopher.

The first involved an attack on Christopher by a rabid dog in 1797. Washington's concern was great enough that he might have allowed himself to be a victim of medical quackery. There was a "hex-doctor" in Lebanon, Pennsylvania, "celebrated for curing persons bitten by mad animals."[118] Washington not only allowed Christopher to travel all the way to Lebanon, Pennsylvania for treatment but also entrusted him with twenty-five dollars, a very significant amount of money in the 18th century, to cover his expenses. In his accompanying letter to the physician, Washington expressed his desire to have Christopher cured. "For besides the call of Humanity, I am particularly anxious for His cure, He being my own Body servant." For whatever reason or reasons, Christopher returned to Mount Vernon cured and declared he no longer feared being bitten by a rabid dog in the future.[119] Interestingly, Washington later noted in his ledger that Christopher returned twelve dollars to him.

Another, darker side of their relationship is indicated in an incident only months before GW's death. Christopher plotted to run away from Mount Vernon. What triggered his decision to flee in

1799 when he had a perfect chance to flee with money in his pocket in 1797 and did not is unknown. Almost certainly his recent marriage to a slave woman from a neighboring plantation was pivotal as she was planning to flee with him. Perhaps the recent marriage of his mother to Charles, a free black man, also influenced him. At any rate, a chance discovery foiled the plot. A note discussing the plan was inadvertently dropped, Washington discovered it, learned of the cabal, and squelched it. [120] (Interestingly, the presence of the note indicates Christopher was literate). Unfortunately, the surviving record leaves no hint of what Washington felt upon learning that his personal servant, on whom he had expended considerable money, wanted to run away. What exchange, if any, occurred between the two men over the planned escape is lost to history. It is, however, perhaps significant that even after learning of the plan to escape, George Washington still kept Christopher as his personal servant, and Christopher was at his post on December 14th.

Equally striking to his concern for those around him was George Washington's remarkable ability to remain "awesomely organized" to the end. Order was always a balm for Washington. Drs. Craik and Dick reported, "during the short period of his illness, he economized his time, in the arrangement of such few concerns as required his attention." His ability to do this while suffering from acute epiglottitis is truly remarkable. If ever a man strove to control and master the environment he found himself in, that man was George Washington.

Washington took seriously and tried to live by the advice he gave his nephew, "Time is limited, that every hour mispent is lost forever." He drove himself, and he drove those around him. He was not an easy man to work for and constantly stressed the need for organization. "System in all things is the soul of business." As he wrote his manager, "Whenever I order a thing to be done, it must be done, or a reason given at the time, or as soon as the impracticality is discovered." [121]

While George Washington's overriding concern had always been "Amor Patriae," he devoted as much time as possible to his personal interests. Washington firmly believed that all men, himself included, were driven by both interest and honor, and while the latter was the more important, Washington was not a selfless altruist unconcerned with his own interests. The result of his drive and ability had been the amassing of a considerable personal fortune, making Washington one of the richest men in America. A major concern was what would happen to this fortune when he was no longer there to oversee the management of it.

The end result of his concern was a remarkable and revealing final will and testament full of detailed instructions which George Washington spent many "leisure hours" composing by himself without the aid of any "professional character" in the summer of 1799. The editors of the newest edition of the Washington Papers noted, the "will was written by a man filled not with forebodings of death but thoughts of the future."[122] His major biographer explained why the writing of the will was so important to him. "Much of the owner and of his forebears was represented in the worldly wealth Washington now contemplated as a whole. His deepest interest and his untiring energy had gone into the acquisition of it; his best efforts had been devoted to the care of it; he must use his best judgment in the disposition of it. In parceling out his possessions, something of himself would be a part of each bequest . . . What he had acquired with ambition and had protected with zeal, he would distribute with infinite care."[123]

In his will he attempted to be as complete and explicit as possible. As he expressed it to Lear the previous year, "My earnest wish and desire being, when I quit the stage of human action, to leave all matters in such a situation as to give as little trouble as possible to those who will have the management of them thereafter." He had been the executor for countless friends and associates and knew what a difficult and thankless task it could be. As he approached death, his "greatest anxiety" was to leave all his own affairs and those of others for whom he was responsible "in such a clear and distinct form . . . that no reproach may attach itself to me when I have taken my departure for the land of spirits."[124]

Late in the afternoon of the 14th, Washington knew his departure was at hand, and he requested his secretary to ask Martha to go downstairs to his study and retrieve two wills from his desk. (It is perhaps noteworthy that Martha was not sitting close enough to her husband to enable him to speak directly to her in his weakened condition). When his wife returned with the wills, the General indicated which was the operative one and requested she burn the other will which she did. Such actions clearly illustrate how Washington seemed to plan for his own death with the same cool precision that he had run his life.

Having taken care of his will, Washington then proceeded to make his longest recorded speech during the entire length of his illness. He spoke to Lear, "I find I am going, my breath can not last long. I believed from the first that the disorder would prove fatal. Do you arrange and record all my late military letters and papers. Arrange my accounts and settle my books, as you know more about them than any one else, and let Mr. Rawlins finish recording my other letters which he has begun." It is not coincidental that George Washington's longest speech, when speech was so very difficult, involved concern with his personal papers.

GW was from the first fascinated with the record of his existence. In W.W. Abbot words, Washington had an "uncommon awareness of self . . . what he decided and what he did, and how others perceived his decisions and deeds always mattered." Abbot demonstrates that this internalized belief of his historical importance is shown most clearly, if indirectly, in his attitude and concern for his papers. [125]

It was a long-standing concern. When it seemed that Lord Dunmore might move against Mount Vernon and perhaps seize Mrs. Washington during the War for Independence, GW requested his manager, Lund Washington, to provide safety "for her and my papers." In late 1776, when the patriot cause looked particularly bleak, he wrote Lund to "have my papers in such a situation as to remove at a short notice in case an Enemy's Fleet should come up the River." At Washington's urging, Congress provided money to have GW's correspondence, orders, and instructions from the war properly arranged and copied into bound volumes, a major undertaking. Sometime in the 1780's, Washington decided it was equally important to arrange his papers from the French and Indian War. As Professor Abbot explains, "finding them marred by awkward constructions, faulty grammar, and misspellings, the hero of the

Revolution proceeded to correct what the young Washington had written more than a quarter of a century before" (although there was no conscious effort to change the meaning of his letters). [126] It was a large undertaking. At the end of his presidency, Washington had his secretaries take from his files what should remain for John Adams, but he shipped the rest to Mount Vernon where he planned to construct a special building on the Mansion farm to house all his papers, both of a public and private nature. (The project was not realized).

This extreme interest and concern for his papers was closely connected to George Washington's desire for fame and secular immortality which were driving forces in his actions. His close aide and friend, David Humphreys, understood his mentor and assured him that his wish would be granted. [127] Washington would not be presumptuous enough or vain enough to write his own story, but he was happy to make available his papers, his home, and his time if his faithful and well-educated aide wished to undertake the effort. A profound concern for his historical reputation was a major aspect of George Washington's character and helps explain his sensitivity to criticism and his desire to avoid reproach.

The authors of the major biography of Washington emphasized another aspect of his character. "The same self-discipline served Washington as patient that had served him as a planter, as Commander-in chief, as President. Duty. . . was his governing principle. . . Today, this 14th of December 1799, he responded as if clearly it was his duty not to deny the doctors and others their valiant efforts to restore him, unavailing though he believed them to be."

In the words of one of his eulogists, Charles Pinckney Sumner, "the calm prescence of mind, with which he had often stood the shock of battle, did not forsake him in his last unequaled triumphant conflict." [128]

Duty and courage were bywords for Washington, and he lived up to his creed. Throughout the entire ordeal the General displayed remarkable fortitude and patience. Grace in the presence of mortal danger comprised a key part of Washington's code of honor, and the ultimate test of honor was courage in the face of death. As Bryan Fairfax wrote to the Earl of Buchan, "Yes, he is gone, but he died, as he lived, with fortitude, so that he was great to the last." In Tobias Lear's word's, "not a complaint escaped him. . . . he died as he lived - fortitude in extreme pain & composure at his latest breath never left him."[129]

George Washington's courage in the face of death is indisputable. The source of that courage is more controversial. To better understand it, a brief look at the death of Virginia's other great popular figure of the 18th century, Patrick Henry, can be instructive. Patrick Henry, suffering from severe intestinal blockage, met his death in June of 1799 with the courage of a convinced Christian. More than a decade earlier he had written his sister on the death of her husband, "This is one of those trying scenes, in which the Christian is eminently superior to all others and finds a refuge which no misfortune can take away." Facing his own imminent demise, Henry used his courage in the face of death as further proof of the truth of the Christian religion. He would go to a place where "sorrows never enter." His wife recounted his death scene in a letter to their daughter, "He met death with firmness and in full confidence that through the merits of a bleeding saviour that his sins would be pardoned."[130]

Although the records of George Washington's final hours are much more comprehensive than those for Henry, they leave a very different picture. While no one can know what Washington was thinking on this subject on December 14th, the complete lack of religious context is striking. According to the extant record of Washington's final hours, there is no reference to any religious words or prayers, no request for forgiveness, no fear of divine judgment, no call for a minister (although ample time existed to call one if desired), no deathbed farewell, no promise or hope of meeting again in Heaven. It is significant that Tobias Lear ended his personal account with the explicit hope that he would meet Washington in Heaven, but his sense of fidelity to a true record kept him from putting such words in Washington's mouth. Martha Washington, a devout Christian, indicated soon afterwards that she hoped to meet her husband in Heaven. (Facing her own death in 1802, Martha found comfort in calling in a clergyman and taking Holy Communion.) Perhaps Washington did not take special leave of any of the family because as Thomas Law wrote, "he had frequently disapproved of the afflicting farewells which aggravated sorrows on those melancholy occasions,"[131] but words of hope of future reunion—if honestly voiced—would surely have given comfort to those left behind.

On this point the privately raised query of the Reverend Samuel Miller, one of Washington's eulogists, is particularly pertinent. "How was it possible, he asked, for a true Christian, in the full exercise of his mental faculties, to die without one expression of distinctive belief, or Christian hope?"[132] George Washington did not draw his courage from a Christian concept of redemption and the hope of eternal bliss through the sacrifice of Christ. Rather, he drew strength from a stoical courage, a strong desire to play his last role on earth's stage in a praise-worthy fashion, and confidence in his virtue and effort to live by the highest ideals. In his words, he had "always walked on a straight line, and endeavoured as far as human frailties, and perhaps strong passions, would enable him, to discharge the relative duties to his Maker and fellow men, without seeking any indirect or left handed attempts to acquire popularity."[133] Finally, and not to be discounted, he was bolstered by his trust in a rather vaguely defined but all-powerful and benign Providence who ultimately controlled human destiny.

In classical stoicism, the true stoic may fall victim to circumstance beyond his control and suffer and perhaps die, but his superior control over his passions calls forth admiration and leads to a reaffirmation of the dignity of man. As Washington's long ordeal continued, and his body weakened under the strain of struggling for air, he somehow drew upon his great inner strength so as to elicit the admiration of those witnessing his struggle.

CHAPTER SIX

WASHINGTON'S DEATH AND FUNERAL

"It is my express desire that my corpse be interred in
a private manner, without parade, or funeral oration."

GEORGE WASHINGTON

As a young man, Washington had boasted, "I have a constitution hardy enough to encounter & undergo the most severe trials." [134] At age sixty-seven he was still surprisingly healthy and vigorous, but George Washington's body could not weather the storm caused by the microscopic invader, and he knew it as clearly as anyone. About 5 o'clock Dr. Craik came again into the room, sat on Washington's bed and gently held his friend's head in his lap. Speaking with difficulty, Washington managed to utter, "Doctor, I am dying, and have been dying for a long time, but I am not afraid to die." [135] Lear recorded the conversation in slightly different form, "Doctor, I die hard; but I am not afraid to go; I believed from my first attack that I should not survive it; my breath can not last long." Craik pressed Washington's hand, but could not utter a word. In a different fashion, Craik's suffering was almost as great as Washington's. He had to face "the most devastating of all duties a doctor is called on to perform—to fight valiantly, yet hopelessly, as death takes a beloved friend." Craik later confessed, "The bonds of my nature were rent aside." [136] Lear noted that the good doctor "retired from the bed side, & sat by the fire absorbed in grief."

Even though they were "without a ray of hope," and despite Washington's heartfelt plea to be allowed to "go off quietly," the physicians found it impossible not to keep trying. Dr. Dick, who had opposed the final bleeding of Washington, proposed a radical course of action to save him. He wanted to perform a tracheotomy, essentially making a hole in the trachea below the obstruction, thus allowing Washington to breathe more easily. Many have expressed their regret that the other physicians overruled him, arguing that it would have saved Washington's life. Over time, Dick became increasingly convinced that the operation should have been performed and particularly singled out Dr. Brown for criticism, although he noted the advanced age and timidity of both of the other physicians. Dick declared, "I shall never cease to regret that the operation was not performed." [137]

Certainly, creating an airway for the General was the number one priority, but one must question the likelihood of its success in this case. In 1799 even elective tracheotomy, let alone emergency tracheotomy, was a near-mythical surgical procedure long footnoted but rarely performed (and almost never in the United States). A workable procedure had been described in surgical detail only the year before. Dr. Dick had never performed such an operation on a live patient although he had recently attempted one on a young five-year-old girl just as she died. His efforts to resuscitate her were unavailing. [138] He would have had to perform the procedure under difficult conditions with poor lighting on a conscious patient in extremis, and on one who had already lost five pints of blood. Because of the airway swelling, forcing GW to lie down would have caused the hugely enlarged epiglottis to fall back and might have obstructed his trachea completely. (Although Dick suggested performing the operation with the patient upright). Secondly, any attempt to give pain relief with laudanum, a derivative of opium that is administered orally and had to be swallowed, might have suppressed Washington's respiration, thus speeding up his demise. Attempting to perform a tracheotomy on an awake semi-sitting patient in extremis without local anesthesia would have been extremely difficult to accomplish even in the best of hands.

Adding to the difficulties, the danger of excessive bleeding from cutting a major blood vessel was significant, and there was a lesser possibility of cutting into the esophagus behind the trachea or puncturing a lung. Furthermore, the chance of the airway collapsing was high since Dr. Dick almost certainly had no tracheotomy tube-like device to keep the opening working. In short, there was a very high probability that the operation would have proved fatal, and one can imagine the public uproar if the great Washington had died as a result of his own physicians slitting his throat. Finally, the evidence clearly indicates that Washington himself was ready "to go," and would not have favored such a heroic measure, a point likely influencing Dr. Craik's final decision. Dr. Dick's idea was therefore rejected, but as late as eight o'clock the doctors still felt compelled to act, and, among other steps, they applied additional blisters to Washington's leg. In Dr. Dick's bitter words, they were acting as a drowning man does who feels impelled "to grasp at a straw."[139] It was to be their final ministration. Washington's long, agonizing struggle was nearing an end.

As the end approached, Washington, a man always desiring to be in control, feared he might be buried alive. (Ironically, he was in fact slowly suffocating, the very thing which would happen to one put in a coffin before they were actually dead.) After several unsuccessful efforts, at last he managed to convey his final request to the faithful Lear. He was not to be buried until he had been dead for at least two days.[140] The idea of being buried alive was a more realistic concern then than it would be today, and the record shows that other members of the Washington family were also worried about it. Hannah Washington, the widow of Washington's favorite brother, John Augustine Washington, was explicit. Referring in her will to the "cruel custom in this country of hurrying a poor creature into a coffin," she declared, "No physician in the world can possibly tell whether a person is dead until putrification takes place and many most assuredly have been buried before they are dead."[141] John Jay had earlier related the story of how he would have been buried alive as a youngster except for the intervention of his mother (It is not clear if GW knew of this story), and later both Bushrod Washington, the inheritor of Mount Vernon, and Washington's own beloved Nelly Custis Lewis warned of the same danger.[142] For whatever reason, the issue was obviously of the utmost importance to Washington. When Lear, choked with emotion, simply nodded, Washington pressed him, "Do you understand me?" Lear said that he did and Washington uttered his last recorded words, "tis well."

Exactly what happened in Washington's final moments on earth is difficult to ascertain. It is possible that Tobias Lear, in his desire for Washington to be rational and in control until the very end of his life, recorded events that Washington had actually done slightly earlier and recounted them as having happened closer to the time of death than they did in fact. Lear noted that shortly before Washington died, "his breathing became easier; he lay quietly." This apparent improvement shortly before death is a trademark of acute epiglottitis, but the reason for the apparent improvement was in all likelihood carbon narcosis, the result of carbon dioxide retention. While lack of oxygen often makes an individual agitated, the build-up of high levels of carbon dioxide serves as a general anesthetic, and the victim eventually lapses into a coma. As this happens, adrenaline levels diminish, the body relaxes and breathing appears easier although in fact complete respiratory failure is approaching.

In Lear's account, George Washington takes his pulse almost immediately before his death. If Washington was in fact in a coma, he would have been unable to perform conscious actions. It is more plausible that as Washington felt himself slipping into a coma he took his own pulse and literally felt the life force ebb out of his great body. We cannot of course know what he was thinking, but about a decade earlier, GW had commented on how he might feel at the time of his death. He would endure the moment by focusing on the positive, especially on his great accomplishment of founding a nation: "Although I shall not live to see but a small portion of the happy effects, which I am confident this system will produce for my Country; yet the precious idea of its prosperity will . . . sooth the mind in the inevitable hour of separation from terrestrial objects."[143]

As Washington lapsed into unconsciousness, he closed his eyes, his hand that had been taking his pulse fell to his side, and for all practical purposes George Washington's life on earth was over. A short time later, Lear, holding tightly to Washington's hand, noticed a change in his countenance and called Dr. Craik to the bedside, and then Washington "expired without a struggle or a sigh." "The great body, which had endured so much, the great mind, so steady in its operation, so sure in its conclusions, was all stilled. Here was no more than an empty vessel, drained for the subsistence of a nation."[144]

His wife, keeping silent and prayerful vigil at the foot of the bed, grasped what had happened. Somehow managing to speak in a firm voice, she asked, "Is he gone?" Lear, struck dumb with grief, could only lift his hand as a way of answering. Echoing her husband's last words, Martha replied in the same tone of voice, "'Tis well. All is now over. I shall soon follow him and I shall rejoice when the moment arrives! I have no more trials to pass through."[145] Certainly, Martha faced the ordeal with courage worthy of the first lady of the land.

Throughout the entire crisis, she had shed no tears. She would not add to his distress by showing her anguish and breaking down.

George Washington was no more. Only the shell of America's "hero, guardian, father, friend" remained. That reality was extremely difficult to accept. As Tobias Lear expressed it the next morning, "While I write I can scarcely believe but it is a dream." [146] In one sense, the mind recognizes the reality but the senses are slow to accept it. The desire to reverse the irreversible was shown most clearly when another close friend and physician, Dr. William Thornton, arrived the next morning. Thornton later recalled his reaction and proposal. "When we arrived, to my unspeakable grief, we found him laid out a stiffened corpse. My feelings at that moment I cannot express! I was overwhelmed with the loss of the best friend I had on Earth. The weather was very cold, and he remained in a frozen state, for several days. I proposed to attempt his restoration, in the following manner. First to thaw him in cold water, then to lay him in blankets, and by degrees and by friction to give him warmth, and to put into activity the minute blood vessels, at the same time to open a passage to the lungs by the trachea, and to inflate them with air, to produce an artificial respiration, and to transfuse blood into him from a lamb." [147] Fortunately, Thornton could not win support for his idea for a posthumous tracheotomy, and Washington's lifeless body was not desecrated.

What should be done with the remains? What should be done to lament the Hero and to honor him? Washington left specific instructions in his will detailing his wishes in this matter: "It is my express desire that my corpse be interred in a private manner, without parade, or funeral oration." At first glance, this wish seems simple and straightforward. However, upon careful inspection, it is ultimately a remarkable and revealing request.

For over twenty years, George Washington had been treated as almost a divine figure. As early as the late 1770's, a Frenchman wrote, "Throughout all [this country] he appears like a benevolent God; old men, women, children all flock eagerly to catch a glimpse of him; people follow him through the towns with torches; his arrival is marked by illuminations." Washington's inaugural trip to New York City in 1789 led to a series of welcomes that treated him almost

as a Messiah. His tours as President of New England and the South confirmed that while Americans were divided on many things, they were virtually unanimous in their admiration, awe, and affection for George Washington. Washington inspired the closest thing to a "cult of personality" that this nation ever witnessed. "Had he lived in the days of idolatry he had been worshipped as a God."[148]

Given his Olympian stature as the "Father of the Country" and the reverence in which he was held by the vast majority of the American people, it was simply inconceivable that the American people would say a final good bye to their "matchless man," their founder and hero, "without parade, or funeral oration." George Washington was an extremely wise and perceptive man. At some level he must have known his death would be a hugely significant event and would spawn numerous elaborate ceremonies. Yet he explicitly stated his desire to be buried in a purely "private," small-scale service. The contrast between the magnitude and intensity of the country's reaction and the low-keyed nature of his request is striking and begs the question, why?

A possible answer to this conundrum lies in the conflict between two central desires motivating Washington: his intense desire to live up to the highest ideals of disinterested service and his intense desire for fame and admiration. One of the most careful studies of Washington's life reveals, "Throughout his life, the ambition for distinction spun inside George Washington like a dynamo . . . Back of George Washington's extraordinary exertions stirred a desire for distinction, a yearning for public esteem that ultimately became a quest for historical immortality. Behind his astounding performance prodded that mixture of egotism and patriotism, selfishness and public-mindedness that historians have come to call the spur of fame."[149] This tension shaped much of Washington's life in ways in which he was often not conscious.

Washington always walked "the tightrope of ambition with fear, and anxiety; afraid that he might slip into self-aggrandizement."[150] He knew that in America diffidence and disinterested service were valued more highly than ambition. His ambition was to win fame for disinterested service to his country. Ultimately, it appears Washington resolved this conflict by convincing himself and his countrymen that he was acting purely out of a desire to promote the interest of his country. Time and time again he announced to the world that his driving motive was that of disinterested service. By making such explicit proclamations, Washington set high standards and made it easier for him to guard against slipping into self-aggrandizement.

The point is that the tension between these two conflicting motives yields a possible answer to Washington's surprising request. As he had numerous times before, he would once again prove to the world—and to himself—that he had acted only for the good of the country, and now that his service to his country was over, he would emphasize his victory over any lusting for fame and glory by specifically requesting that he be buried in a purely private ceremony. The request would comport with the world's image of him and his image of himself. Yet, Washington almost certainly knew that this was one request which would be denied him, and at a very deep level, Washington likely hoped it would not be carried out. If it were not, Washington would be in the enviable position of remaining true to his values of disinterested service and still have his craving for admiration and fame realized. (See note 151 for a slightly different interpretation.)

The word of the General's death spread with great rapidity. By Monday the 16th, all the shops of Alexandria were shut, the bells were tolling, and everyone appeared in black or with crepe. It quickly became clear that a purely private ceremony was simply not feasible. The people of his beloved Alexandria and the surrounding environs felt a compelling need to be part of the final farewell to their favorite son, and a small funeral would not allow that to happen. Whatever the ultimate size of the funeral would be, however, preparations had to begin almost immediately. The body had to be washed and prepared, most likely by Christopher, and laid out in the large dining room in the north wing of the mansion, the very room where Washington had received word of his unanimous election as America's first president a decade earlier. Dr. Dick carefully noted Washington measurements so that the correct size coffin could be built.

6'3 1/2" length exact
1'9" across shoulders exact
2'9" across elbows exact."

Lear, controlling his personal grief, was tireless in sending letters to key people from the President of the United States to family members, informing them of Washington's death. While Washington lay on his death bed, Lear had sent off hurried notes to Mrs. Law and Mrs. Peter and their husbands (Eliza Custis Law and Martha Custis Peter, granddaughters of Mrs. Washington, both lived in the Federal City, now Washington, D.C.). They arrived at Mount Vernon on the 15th. There was a desire to delay the funeral service until Nelly's brother, George Washington Parke Custis, and her husband, Lawrence Lewis, could attend, (Washington had asked about their return while on his death bed), but in view of the inflammatory nature of Washington's disease and fear of contagion, it was decided to hold the funeral on Wednesday, December 18th at noon, and Lear sent letters to close neighbors inviting them to the sad occasion.

Funeral preparations allowed those closest to Washington to repress their grief through activities. Martha Washington took an active part in the planning and remained stoically calm on the surface. In the words of Thomas Law, she "displayed a solemn composure that was more distressing than floods of tears." Her faith strengthened her hope that she would soon "be again united with the partner of my life." Still, she was devastated and indicated that she viewed her life on earth as essentially over. She informed Law that she would now not see their home in the new capital city named for her husband because she would never leave Mount Vernon again. [152] She requested Tobias Lear not to seal up the family vault because she fully expected (and one could add, desired) to join her husband there shortly. Lear later recalled that he was almost frantically busy, but explained to his mother that the duty he owed Washington's memory kept him from yielding to immoderate grief in the days leading up to the funeral.

Bills still in the possession of Mount Vernon give an indication of the many activities occurring. [153] At Martha's request, Lear went into Alexandria on Sunday the 15th to make arrangements for a coffin. He settled on a mahogany coffin lined with black lace with a silver engraved plate:

General

George Washington

Departed this life on the 14th of December

1799, Aet. 68

The coffin was adorned with two commonly used inscriptions: Surge Ad Judicium (Rise Up to Be Judged) and Gloria Deo (Glory to God). At the insistence of William Thornton the coffin was enclosed in lead, for when Thornton had composed the plan and elevation of the Capitol of the U.S. he designed the dome for Washington's mausoleum and wanted the body preserved so it would not disintegrate over time. The charges for the coffin and sundry items such as rental of the bier was $99.25 while the charge for "leading a coffin" was £14 10s. A shroud and extra mourning candles were also purchased.

To receive the coffin, the old family vault, built at Lawrence Washington's request many years earlier, was opened and cleaned on the 16th. Washington recognized the poor condition of the old family vault in his will. "The family Vault at Mount Vernon requiring repairs, and being improperly situated besides, I desire a new one of Brick, and upon a larger scale, may be built at the foot of what is commonly called the Vineyard Inclosure,—on the ground which is marked out.—In which my remains, with those of my deceased relatives (now in the Old Vault) and such others of my family as may chuse to be entombed there, may be deposited." (Rather surprisingly, this request was not actually honored for over thirty years). The coffin arrived at Mount Vernon at about one o'clock on the 17th. Lear described it, "The Mahogany Coffin was lined with lead, soddered at the joints—and a cover of lead to be soddered on after the body should be in the Vault. The whole was put into a case lined & covered with black Cloth."

The Mansion House needed many items as the mourning began. A bill from Forsyth and Smith lists some of them: 32 yards of black ribbon, 600 white tacks, 3 yards superfine black cloth, 72 yards narrow black ribbon, 16 yards black crepe, 18 yards Irish linen for scarves. Mourning clothes had to be purchased for both the family and for the house servants and interestingly, the charges were the same for mourning clothes for Christopher and the other house servants as they were for Lawrence Lewis and George Washington Parke Custis. Christopher was also given new shoes to improve his appearance with so many guests expected. (Washington would undoubtedly have approved since he always firmly believed that appearances matter.) Provisions had to be procured for the expected large number of mourners. Forty pounds of pound cake and three large cheeses weighing a total of sixty-one pounds were ordered. Mount Vernon's own distillery sent twenty-nine gallons of whiskey to the Mansion House, and George Gilpin supplied ten gallons of spirits on the 17th.

Plans for the actual funeral had to be worked out. George Washington's Masonic Lodge, Number 22, insisted on saying a formal farewell to their most distinguished member with full Masonic rites and met at their Alexandria lodge to plan the ceremony. In addition, the militia wanted to give a military salute to their former commander. The day before the internment, Lt. John Stewart, Adjutant of the 106th Regiment of Virginia Militia and aide to Colonel George Deneale who was to lead the military, arrived at Mount Vernon to view the ground for the procession.

On the morning of the 18th the open coffin was placed on Mount Vernon's magnificent piazza, which George Washington had designed and from which he had on so many occasions looked out at the magnificent Potomac River which flowed past a few hundred yards away. Mourners silently filed past the coffin for one last look at Washington's earthly remains. The Virginia Herald printed a letter from Georgetown written on the 20th: "In the long & lofty Portico where oft the hero walked in all his glory, now lay the shrouded corpse—The countenance still composed & serene, seemed to express the dignity of the spirit which lately dwelt in the lifeless form. . . . There those who paid the last sad honors to the benefactor of his country took an impressive farewell view." [154] While scheduled for noon, difficulty in assembling the troops delayed the actual beginning of the service until about 3 p.m.

Tobias Lear described the route, "The procession moved out of the Gate at the left Wing of the House, and proceeded round in front of the lawn, & down to the Vault on the right wing of the

House." The procession was accompanied by a band playing a solemn dirge augmented by muffled drums and the firing of minute guns from a schooner on the Potomac River. The cavalry led the procession, followed by the infantry and the guard, all with arms reversed. Then followed four clergymen, and behind them was the General's riderless horse carrying Washington's saddle, holster and pistols, led by two servants, Cyrus and Wilson, in full mourning.

Washington's coffin on a bier was borne by members of the militia and six honorary pallbearers. Following the bier were the principal mourners, including some family members and close friends like Bryan Fairfax, Dr. Craik and Lear. Martha Washington did not attend the funeral for reasons that are not clear. She had maintained a stoic composure throughout the ordeal and would not cry until many weeks later. She may have been too grief stricken to attend and there is no doubt about the depth of her affliction, but there may have been some other personal reasons, including custom, that led to her decision. It is worth noting that none of her three granddaughters attended either. Indeed, the procession was overwhelmingly male. Following the principal mourners came a large contingent of Masons from several lodges but primarily from Washington's home lodge, and then the rest of the "vast concourse" of people led by Washington's manager, John Anderson and his overseers, and including at least some of his slaves.

Arriving at the burial site, the Reverend Thomas Davis read the Order of Burial from the Episcopal Prayer Book, and Dr. Elisha Dick, as the Worshipful Master of GW's Masonic Lodge, aided by Rev. James Muir, the Lodge's chaplain, conducted full Masonic rites. Washington's Masonic apron and sword were removed from the coffin and "the brethren one by one cast upon it an evergreen sprig," symbolizing their hope in the resurrection. The coffin was lowered and the final words were spoken: 'Earth to earth—ashes to ashes—dust to dust," and the entombment of Washington was over. [155] As the ceremony ended, three general discharges of the infantry, the cavalry, and eleven pieces of artillery in the woods behind the vault in concert with the minute guns from the schooner paid the final tribute to the fallen commander.

By all accounts the service was a moving one for all involved.

George Washington was interred in the family tomb with great ceremony on the afternoon of December 18, 1799.

Thomas Law informed his brother, "yesterday the cavalry Rifle men Militia Artillery & Free Masons with a vast concourse of people attended—the solemn music the minute Guns from an armed vessel on the River the slow march of the troops with arms reversed and the long procession formed a most awful Scene." Another reported, "We have all of us been crying ever since, and at the funeral there was not one dry eye among the thousands of people who gathered to render him the honors....there were soldiers, but otherwise everything was quite simple." One of the attending Masons noted, "As I helped place his body in the vault, and stood at the door while the funeral service was performing, I had the best opportunity of observing the countenances of all. Everyone was affected, but none so much as his domestics of all ages." [156] "Everyone was affected"! Those living near Mount Vernon were able to come to the funeral services and openly grieve and pay tribute. Distance made that option impossible for the vast majority of the nation, but as word of Washington's death spread like wildfire, the American people seemed to react as one as they sought to come to grips with the sudden loss of their founder and greatest champion.

CHAPTER SEVEN

GRIEVING FOR A FALLEN HERO

"On this occasion it is manly to weep."

TOBIAS LEAR

It is difficult to exaggerate the impact George Washington's death had on the American people. It was a cataclysmic event in the life of the young republic. Benjamin Rush, one of Washington's more severe critics, admitted that it was as if a large part of the country all lost their father at exactly the same time. (See note 157 for brief comment on partisanship) The resulting grief was profound and overwhelming as individuals and communities sought to come to grips with the loss of what many viewed as their most sacred possession. The following examples, which could be multiplied many times over, give an accurate sense of the mood among much of the country.

"I felt, and I was witness, on the day when the news of his death reached us, to the throes of that grief, that saddened every countenance, and wrung drops of agony from the heart. Sorrow labored for utterance but found none. Every man looked round for the consolation of other men's tears. Gracious Heaven! What consolation! Each face was convulsed with sorrow for the past, every heart shivered with despair for the future. The man, who and whom alone, united all hearts, was dead." [158]

"We were most dreadfully shocked last Wednesday at the account of the Death of the Dear old gen'l oh! How we have bewailed his loss;—the father of his C; you know not my Dear Mamma how this event has distroyed me, it haunts my slumbers and the ye day I can think of Nothing else." [159]

"Undissembled grief has been depicted on every countenance, where the news of General Washington's death has arrived." [160]

"Washington is gone! Ah, fatal night in which he fell! Let darkness seize upon it—Let it not be joined unto the days of the year—Let it not come into the number of the months. Lo, let that night be solitary—Let no joyful voice come near it. Such are the effusions of inconsolable grief, in the first transports of pardonable excess." [161]

"Still be the Voice of Mirth! Hushed be all Sounds of Joy! In silent sorrow, mourn, Columbia, mourn! If loss of worth unequaled here below, be cause of grief or cause of woe and grief unbounded, bides thee mourn, thy worthiest, noblest Son is no more— ILLUSTRIOUS WASHINGTON is dead!" [162]

Many found it difficult if not impossible to adequately express the grief they felt. Touchingly, one recipient of Lear's letter bearing the ill tidings responded by sending back a letter without a single line on it, "the blank expressing more forcibly than words the excess of his grief." [163] However difficult to do adequately, most people felt compelled to attempt to express their grief. Americans were requested to wear a badge of crepe, and nearly all did so. Dwellings and theaters were hung in black, newspapers were black bordered, and the bells tolled mournfully and long in almost every town. Black cloth was hard to buy in Massachusetts as late as July of the following year. Since most were unable to attend GW's actual funeral, they sought comfort in elaborate mock funerals complete with pallbearers, biers, and urns, and in numerous processions, memorial services, and eulogies.

In Philadelphia, then the nation's capital, Congress immediately adjourned on hearing the news mournfully announced by John Marshall. They quickly adopted various resolutions such as shrouding the Speaker's chair in black and having members and officers of the house wear black during the remainder of the session. President Adams, despite his ambivalent feelings for his predecessor, declared, "I felt myself alone, bereft of my last brother," and ordered the military to wear mourning for six months. In passing on Adams' order, Alexander Hamilton, himself feeling bereft by the death of his "kind and unchanging friend," confided to the troops, "Tis only for me to mingle my tears with those of my fellow soldiers." [164] December 26th was declared the official day of mourning for the city.

Philadelphia mourned in an immense and somber show of state—a grim parade of virtually the entire Congress, the judiciary, the Cabinet, municipal officials, 33 clergymen wearing white scarves, and Major General Alexander Hamilton, trailed by a vast train of the

Cincinnati veterans, many different militia units, a band playing a solemn dirge, and "citizens" in a nine-block-walk through sodden weather from Congress Hall to the German Lutheran Church where a mob of 4,000 jammed into the church and sat in tears through a two-hour oration by Henry Lee extolling the man who was "first in war, first in peace, and first in the hearts of his countrymen." Prominent in the procession—and also drawing sobs from the 10,000 who thronged the parade route—was a white stallion, trimmed in black, its head festooned with elegant black and white feathers with the American Eagle displayed in a rose on its breast and in a feather on its head, bearing Washington's saddle, holster, and pistols (with boots dramatically reversed). The immense black-draped and empty coffin followed with the General's hat and sword, borne by four sergeants and six honorary pall bearers as if it contained the body of the hero, now eight days in his tomb. [165]

A good example of one smaller town's grief, replicated with modifications around the country, is the account of the mourning in the town of Charlestown, near Boston. "At Charlestown, on Tuesday last, funeral honors were paid to the memory of Washington. Every class of citizen suspended their occupations to mingle their tears at such a berefting ceremony—As the procession entered the church, the organ played a solemn dirge—every heart was in unison with the melancholy peal. Dr. Morse arose & prayed. Humility, devotion, grief, resignation, and joyful hope fell[?] alternately upon his countenance, and animated his voice. During his pathetic apostrophe the shade of our beloved Hero seemed to be hovering in the midst. After an appropriate hymn, Dr. Morse addressed the assembly in an elegant and feeling discourse. The saint and the patriot, the American and christian were here conspicuous. Solemn music formed an interlude between the sermon & Washington's inestimable legacy [Farewell Address]. Though dead, our beloved chief seemed yet to speak — not from the grave but from Heaven. At the conclusion of this [,] night approached. At this season, when every object was suited to inspire a melancholy awe, the service was concluded with a funeral dirge. A full choir chaunted [sic] this solemn requiem, every one seemed to feel it to be the last adieu—responsive sighs heaved every bosom—the big tear stood in every eye—the organ ceased, and every heart groaned amen!" [166]

As one modern scholar expressed it, "Everywhere these ceremonies melded religious, ethnic, political, and economic factors into a moral unity." In death, as he was in life, GW was to be "the man who unites all hearts." Americans saw Washington as much more than an esteemed role model: he was, in the most literal sense, a sacred possession.[167] Between his death in December and February 22, 1800, the major final day of official mourning, at least 440 funeral elegies honoring Washington were presented around the country, and a great many of them have survived. The image which emerges from them is, as Tobias Lear suspected, one of a man who appears "to be more than a man."

At Harvard College, GW was numbered among the "gods of the earth," while more subtly, Phillips Payson did not recollect "ever hearing of a single instance of mistake, error, or blame, that was ever justly charged upon him." "Well may he be ranked," preached David Tappan, "among Earthly Gods, who, to other great accomplishments united a 'humble', yet near resemblance of HIM, who is the standard of human perfection and the EXPRESS IMAGE of divine glory." So extreme were some of the comparisons that many clergymen expressed fear that America had provoked the envy of God Himself. Even Dr. William Thornton, who wrote, "I believe no sorrow for his loss is more real than my own," worried about the tendency to deify Washington and make him into a god/man. "I have seen late orations which instead of being sublime are absolutely in some places bombastically impious."[168]

GW was compared favorably to all the outstanding biblical, classical and modern heroes, but no analogy was so well developed as the contention that the departed leader had truly been a Moses for America. "As the deliverer and political savior of our nation, he has been the same to us, as Moses was to the Children of Israel." Indeed, to many, Washington was even superior to Moses. After all, Washington completed his task while Moses died just short of his fulfillment. Moses brought the Israelites within sight of the Promised Land, but Washington "saw his country's glory finished."[169]

As the reality of Washington's passing settled in on the American people, they desperately sought consolation in the midst of grief. As Alexander Hamilton wrote to Tobias Lear, "For great misfortunes it is the business of reason to seek consolation. The friends of General W. have very noble ones. If virtue can secure happiness in another world he is happy. In this [his death] the Seal is now put upon his glory. It is no longer in jeopardy from the fickleness of fortune." [170] Hamilton's final point, the theme of secured glory, was a major one as people sought comfort and reassurance.

For example, Bishop James Madison, giving what turned to be one of the most often quoted and influential eulogies, properly chose as his text, Second Timothy: 4.7: "I have fought a good fight. I have finished the course." As Richard Brookhiser notes, the Senate got it exactly right about George Washington. "The scene is closed — and we are no longer anxious lest misfortune should sully his glory; he has traveled on to the end of his journey, and carried with him an increasing weight of honor: he has deposited it safely where misfortune can not tarnish it; where malice can not blast it." [171] Certainly, Washington had feared, almost irrationally so unless one remembers how important his reputation was to him, that he would do something which might justly lower himself in the esteem of the American people. While unlikely, such an event might have happened if he had lived.

As maneuvering for the presidential campaign of 1800 heated up, partisan wrangling between the Federalists and the Republicans increased. During the last months of 1799, the conviction grew among increasing numbers of Federalists that John Adams was not the man for the job nor could he win re-election, and there was a growing move to draft GW once more to stand for the presidency. A powerful letter from one of GW's more intimate associates, Gouverneur Morris, urging him to run, arrived as Washington's cold body lay in the dining room awaiting burial. Had he lived, would Washington have in time succumbed to the increasing pressure to come out of retirement one more time to save the country from disaster? Earlier in the year, he had been adamant in his refusal to consider it, but at other times in his life he had been equally adamant and then had changed his mind due to a sense of obligation and duty. Had he been convinced his service was needed again for the good of the country, might he have done so again? John Adams, who knew Washington well, later wrote he believed that Washington "expected to be called in again, as he certainly would have been had he lived." [172] Clearly, Adams' assertion is purely speculative, might have been a reflection of his personal bitterness, and may not be accurate.

Nevertheless, one of GW's greatest and most enduring gifts to the young nation had been his voluntary withdrawal from power, both at the end of the War for Independence and again after his second term as President. His eulogists stressed this point over and over. If, at his advanced age and at a time of diminishing competency, Washington had been re-elected President and died in office, the value of that example would have been severely diminished. His sudden death made the question simply one of conjecture and ensured that his fame would not be tarnished. In that sense, he died at a fortuitous time.

The idea of Washington finishing his increasingly difficult course with his honor completely intact helped the people cope with their grief. The Earl of Buchan sought to console Martha Washington along those lines by quoting Tacitus concerning Agricola, "That tho' he was snatched away whilst his age was not yet broken by infirmity or diminished by bodily decay of reason yet that if his life be measured by glory, he attained to a mighty length of days." [173]

While it may not have been completely accurate, the shared perception first promulgated by Lear was that Washington had maintained his reason until the very end of his life. Thomas Law assured his brother, "when he was near expiring he asked the hour felt his pulse and closed his eyes and left this world without a sigh or groan." S. Lyman informed his wife on Jan 7, 1800 that Dr. Craik "wrote a gentleman in this City, that the General, with his own fingers, closed his own Eyes in death — this circumstance is a little remarkable, and it showed that he had his reason, and a spirit of resignation. . . such was the death of this great man." [174]

Whether exactly accurate or not, the truth of the matter was that George Washington died as he had lived. He was in fact the man he appeared to be. He left a priceless legacy for the nation he loved and did so much to bring into creation. President Adams urged Americans to "teach their children never to forget that the fruit of his labors & his example are their inheritance." Gouverneur Morris, who knew Washington well and wrote perhaps the most perceptive of all the Washington eulogies, attempted to make sense of his death by closing his tribute with these words. "Wonderful man! he seems immortal—Oh no—No—No, this our pride, our glory is gone—He is gone forever. . . . And yet his spirit liveth—He liveth—he shall live forever!" [175]

Appendix

Tobias Lear's Account of the Death of George Washington

"This day being marked by an event which will be memorable in the History of America, and perhaps of the World, I shall give a particular statement of it, to which I was an eye witness."

Tobias Lear

Since Tobias Lear is the primary narrator of Washington's death, a crucial question revolves around the accuracy and reliability of his account. Certainly, as was indicated above, Tobias Lear was not simply an uninterested bystander. He cannot be compared with the person who happens to witness an accident but has no connection with those involved and no stake in the results of the investigation.

In time, Tobias Lear's admiration for Washington came close to reverence. After being his private secretary for a few years, Lear assessed Washington in these words: "General Washington is, I believe, almost the only man of an exalted character who does not lose some part of his respectability by an intimate acquaintance. I have lived with him near two years, . . . and I declare I have never found a single thing which could lessen my respect for him. A complete knowledge of his honesty, uprightness and candor in all his private transactions, has sometimes led me to think he is more than a man." [176]

Clearly, Tobias Lear is not an "objective" witness. The key question is how reliable a witness is he? The answer is that, with certain significant qualifications, he is a reliable witness. In the first place, Lear was a gifted reporter. Intelligent and well educated, he wrote with vigor and clarity. Washington thought him an excellent reporter and declared he was "one from whom you may obtain the best oral information of the real state of matters in this Country." [177] Washington demonstrated his confidence by sending Lear on a twenty-eight day mission to check on his western land holdings for him.

Tobias Lear was an eyewitness to the accounts he described. He was at Washington's side and bedside throughout that long and trying day. It is important to remember that there is a tremendous vividness to a deathbed scene such as Lear witnessed. While one might confuse certain details or confuse exactly when particular events transpired (and there is evidence this happened), one will nevertheless remember the events themselves vividly. Significantly strengthening the account's reliability, Lear wrote about the incidents he witnessed almost immediately after they occurred. He penned his "journal" entry on the very next day, December 15, as well as writing individuals close to the president informing them of his death. On the 16th he wrote a description of the events in a purely private letter to his mother which he told her not to make public. Lear, because of exhaustion and his own agitated state of mind, expressed uncertainty as to what he had included in the letter. Nevertheless, this private letter closely agrees with what he said both earlier and later. Additionally, two of the three attending physicians, Doctors James Craik and Elisha Cullen Dick, wrote their own brief account (it was actually composed by Dr. Dick) of Washington's final hours within days of his death. While much shorter and different in emphasis, theirs' being primarily a medical account, it generally supports Lear's account, differing slightly on things such as the arrival of the physicians and the time of death. [178] Thomas Law, the husband of Washington's step-granddaughter, Eliza Parke Custis, arrived the day after Washington had died and stayed at Mount Vernon through the funeral three days later. An interesting letter written over the four-day period to his brother in England, often cited above, further corroborates Lear's view, and adds a few new details. [179]

Later in the month, Lear wrote a longer "diary" account, which in some minor respects varies from his shorter "journal" account of the 15th. [180] While there are slight differences and discrepancies between the two versions, the second, larger version, which carries the story up until the time GW's coffin was sealed on December 25th, simply appears to be an effort to augment the account given very shortly after Washington's death so as to include more information while it was still fresh in Lear's memory. It is worth noting that Dr. James Craik later endorsed the larger "diary" account as accurate "as far as I can recollect."

Furthermore, there is nothing inherently implausible in the account, even if particular points may be in dispute. By way of contrast, the famous and often used account of Washington's final hours by Mason 'Parson' Weems is replete with implausible assertions, including the words of a completely private prayer Washington supposedly uttered after he sent everyone out of the room, and is not to be trusted as an accurate source. [181] In fact, the things which are not included in Lear's narrative strengthen the case for its veracity. There are, for example, no final patriotic or religious quotes included, no special farewell words for Lear or any of the others at his bedside. Indeed, according to Lear, Washington's final—and heartfelt—worry was that he would be buried alive. It would be most unlikely for Lear to include this incident unless it happened as, while not embarrassing, it does not portray Washington in a particularly heroic fashion. Contrast this with Weems' account of Washington's last words— "Father of mercies! take me to thyself."

Admittedly, in Lear's account as a whole, Washington faced death in a very admirable—indeed perhaps heroic—fashion, but at several other well-documented points in his life Washington had faced death in just such a fashion. It certainly does not strain credulity to believe that, consistent with the human reaction to pain and difficulty breathing, Washington faced his final challenge in the same way. Indeed, when one realizes how important it was to Washington to meet his final challenge "with grace," his actions were not implausible but consistent with the entire tenor of his life.

Nevertheless, despite all the positive aspects about the Lear account, it cannot be accepted uncritically. Certainly, Lear's account is not complete. He naturally focuses on what he is doing to the partial exclusion of others like Mrs. Washington and Dr. Craik, and Washington probably had more contact and communication with them than Lear's account indicates. Undoubtedly, other things happened during that long day which he either forgot or chose not to include. Did certain events occur which Lear deliberately chose not to include because they were at odds with his portrayal of Washington's heroic and rational death? Did he have Washington say and do things that he did not say or do? While a categorical answer is difficult, there is no certain evidence to support such claims.

Nonetheless, Lear clearly sanitized Washington's death and

downplayed the most horrific aspects of it. The inevitable terror connected with gasping for air was omitted. Being unable to swallow or having great difficulty in swallowing would inevitably have caused Washington to drool. The nose and mouth, through mucus-secreting glands and salivary glands, produce an average of two quarts of fluid per day.[182] If one is unable to swallow without choking, this fluid will be forcibly ejected out of the nose or out of the mouth or both, but Lear, perhaps because of the image such a report would conjure up for his readers, does not specifically report it. Probably for similar reasons of delicacy, Lear in his original account omits any reference to a discharge from the bowels. In his revised addition, and after Drs. Dick and Craik had specifically referred to it in their widely read account, Lear then included it. There is some evidence, discussed above, that Washington's actions reported by Lear to take place at the moment of GW's death may actually have happened slightly earlier.

But if Lear is not the absolute and definitive word, the chronicle, strengthened by Lear's natural gift as a reporter, is still priceless. It opens a window on this event which otherwise would be essentially closed and allows us a close-up view of how George Washington confronted his final struggle. Reproduced below is Lear's longer "diary" account up to the time of the General's body being laid out in the great dining room at Mount Vernon.

On Thursday Decr. 12th. the General rode out to his farms about ten o'clock, and did not return home till past three. Soon after he went out the weather became very bad, rain, hail, and snow falling alternately with a cold wind: When he came in, I carried some letters to him to frank, intending to send them to the Post-Office in the evening. He franked the letters; but said the Weather was too bad to send a servant to the Office that evening. I observed to him that I was afraid he had got wet; he said no, his great Coat had kept him dry; but his neck appeared to be wet, and the snow was hanging upon his hair. He came to dinner (which had been Waiting for him) without changing his dress. In the evening he appeared as well as usual.

A heavy fall of snow took place on Friday (which prevented the General from riding out as usual.) He had taken cold (undoubtedly from being so much exposed the day before) and complained of a sore throat: he however went out in the afternoon into the ground between the House and the River to mark some trees which were to be cut down in the improvement of that spot. He had a Hoarseness which increased in the evening; but he made light of it. In the evening the Papers were brought from the Post Office, and he sat in the Parlour, with Mrs. Washington & myself reading them till about nine o'clock—when Mrs. W. went up into Mrs. Lewis's room, who was confined in Child Bed, and left the General & myself reading the papers. He was very cheerful and when he met with anything interesting or entertaining, he wd. read it aloud as well as his hoarseness would permit him. He requested me to read to him the debates of the Virginia Assembly on the election of a Senator and a Governor;—and on hearing Mr. Madison's observations respecting Mr. Monroe, he appeared much affected and spoke with some degree of asperity on the subject, which I endeavoured to moderate, as I always did on such occasions. On his retiring I observed to him that he had better take something to remove his cold. He answered no; "you know I never take any thing for a cold. Let it go as it came."

Between two & three o'clock on Saturday morning, he awoke

Mrs. Washington, and told her he was very unwell, and had had an ague. She observed that he could scarcely speak and breathed with difficulty; and would have got up to call a Servant; but he would not permit her lest she should take cold. As soon as the day appeared, the Woman (Caroline) went into the Room to make a fire, and Mrs. Washington sent her immediately to call me. I got up, put on my clothes as quickly as possible, and went to his Chamber. Mrs. Washington was then up, and related to me his being taken ill as before stated. I found the General breathing with difficulty, and hardly able to utter a word intelligibly. He desired that Mr. Rawlins (one of the overseers) might be sent for to bleed him before the Dr. could arrive. I dispatched a servant instantly for Rawlins, and another for Dr. Craik, and returned again to the General's Chamber, where I found him in the same situation as I had left him. A mixture of Molasses, Vinegar & butter was prepared to try its effects in the throat; but he could not swallow a drop. Whenever he attempted it he appeared to be distressed, convulsed and almost suffocated. Rawlins came in soon after sun rise, and prepared to bleed him. When the arm was ready the General observing that Rawlins appeared to be agitated, said, as well as he could speak "Don't be afraid." And after the incision was made, he observed, " The orifice is not large enough." However the blood ran pretty freely. Mrs. Washington not knowing whether bleeding was proper or not in the General's situation, begged that much might not be taken from him, lest it should be injurious, and desired me to stop it; but when I was about to untie the string the General put up his hand to prevent it, and as soon as he could speak, said— "More, more." Mrs. Washington being still very uneasy lest too much blood should be taken, it was stopped after taking about half a pint. Finding that no relief was obtained from bleeding, and that nothing would go down the throat, I proposed bathing it externally with salvolatila, which was done; and in the operation, which was with the hand, and in the gentlest manner, he observed "tis very sore." A piece of flannel dip'd in salvolatila was put around his neck, and his feet bathed in warm water; but without affording any relief.

In the mean time, before Dr. Craik arrived Mrs. Washington desired me to send for Dr. Brown of Post Tobacco, whom Dr. Craik had recommended to be called, if any case should ever occur that was seriously alarming. I dispatched a messenger (Cyrus) immediately for Dr. Brown (between 8 & 9 o'clock). Dr. Craik came in soon after, and upon examining the General, he put a blister of Cantharides on the throat, took some more blood from him, and had a gargle of Vinegar & sage tea, and ordered some Vinegar and hot water for him to inhale the steam which he did;—but in attempting to use the gargle he was almost suffocated. When the gargle came from his throat some phlegm followed it, and he attempted to Cough, which the Doctor encouraged him to do as much as possible; but he could only attempt it. About eleven o'clock Dr. Craik requested that Dr. Dick might be sent for, as he feared Dr. Brown would not come in time. A messenger was accordingly dispatched for him. About this time the General was bled again. No effect however was produced by it, and he remained in the same state, unable to swallow anything. A blister was administered about 12 o'clock, which produced an evacuation; but caused no alteration in his complaint.

Dr. Dick came in about 3 o'clock, and Dr. Brown arrived soon after. Upon Dr. Dick's seeing the General and consulting a few minutes with Dr. Craik he was bled again; the blood came very slow, was thick, and did not produce any symptoms of fainting. Dr. Brown came into the chamber soon after; and upon feeling the General's pulse &c. the Physicians went out together. Dr. Craik returned soon after. The General could now swallow a little. Calomel & tarter em. were administered, but without any effect.

About half past 4 o'clock he desired me to call Mrs. Washington to his bed side, when he requested her to go down into his room, and take from his desk two Wills which she would find there, and bring them to him, which she did. Upon looking at them he gave her one which he observed was useless, as being superseded by the other, and desired her to burn it, which she did, and took the other and put it into her Closet.

After this was done, I returned to his bed side, and took his hand. He said to me, "I find I am going, my breath can not last long. I believed from the first that the disorder would prove fatal. Do you arrange and record all my late military letters and papers. Arrange my accounts and settle my books, as you know more about them than any one else, and let Mr. Rawlins finish recording my other letters which he has begun." I told him this should be done. He then asked if I recollected anything which it was essential for him to do, as he had but a very short time to continue among us. I told him I could recollect nothing; but that I hoped he was not so near his end; he observed smiling, that he certainly was, and that as it was the debt that all must pay, he looked to the event with perfect resignation.

In the course of the afternoon he appeared to be in great pain and distress, from the difficulty of breathing, and frequently changed his position in the bed. On these occasions I lay upon the bed, and endeavoured to raise him, and turn him with as much care as possible. He appeared penetrated with gratitude for my attentions, & often said, I am afraid I shall fatigue you too much, and upon my assuring him that I could feel nothing but a wish to give him ease, he replied, "Well it is a debt we must pay to each other, and I hope when you want aid of this kind you will find it."

He asked when Mr. Lewis & Washington Custis would return, (they were in New Kent) I told him about the 20th. of the month.

About 5 o'clock Dr. Craik came again into the room & upon going to the bed side the Genl. said to him, Doctor, I die hard; but I am not afraid to go; I believed from my first attack that I should not survive it; my breath can not last long.

The Doctor pressed his hand, but could not utter a word. He retired from the bed side, & sat by the fire absorbed in grief.

Between 5 & 6 o'clk Dr. Dick & Dr. Brown came into the room, and with Dr. Craik went to the bed; when Dr. Craik asked him if he could sit up in the bed? He held out his hand & I raised him up. He then said to the Physicians, "I feel myself going, I thank you for your attentions; but I pray you to take no more trouble about me, let me go off quietly, I can not last long." They found that all which had been done was without effect; he laid down again and all retired except Dr. Craik. He continued in the same situation, uneasy & restless, but without complaining; frequently asking what hour it was. When I helped him to move at this time he did not speak, but looked at me with strong expressions of gratitude.

About 8 o'clock the Physicians came again into the room and applied blisters and cataplasms of wheat bran to his legs and feet; after which they went out (except Dr. Craik) without a ray of hope. I went out about this time and wrote a line to Mr. Law & Mr. Peter, requesting them to come with their wives (Mrs. Washington's Granddaughters) as soon as possible to Mt Vernon.

About ten o'clk he made several attempts to speak to me before he could effect it, at length he said,—"I am just going. Have me decently buried; and do not let my body be put into the Vault in less than three days after I am dead." I bowed assent, for I could not speak. He then looked at me again and said, "Do you understand me? I replied "Yes." "Tis well" said he.

About ten minutes before he expired (which was between ten & eleven o 'clk) his breathing became easier; he lay quietly;—he withdrew his hand from mine, and felt his own pulse. I saw his countenance change. I spoke to Dr. Craik who sat by the fire;—he came to the bed side. The General's hand fell from his wrist—I took it in mine and put it into my bosom. Dr. Craik put his hands over his eyes and he expired without a struggle or a sigh!

While we were fixed in silent grief, Mrs. Washington (who was sitting at the foot of the bed) asked with a firm & collected voice, Is he gone? I could not speak, but held up my hand as a signal that he was no more. 'Tis well, said she in the same voice, "All is now over I shall soon follow him! I have no more trials to pass through!"

Occurrences not noted in the preceding narrative

The General's servant Christopher was in the room through the day; and in the afternoon the General directed him to sit down, as he had been standing almost the whole day; he did so.

About 8 o'clock in the morning he expressed a desire to get up. His clothes were put on and he was led to a chair by the fire. He found no relief from this position, and lay down again about 10 o'clk. About 5 P.M. he was helped up again & after sitting about half an hour desired to be undressed & put in bed; which was done.

During his whole illness he spoke but seldom, and with great difficulty; and in so low & broken a voice as at times hardly to be understood. His patience, fortitude, & resignation never forsook him for a moment. In all his distress he uttered not a sigh, nor a complaint; always endeavouring (from a sense of duty as it appeared) to take what was offered him, and to do as he was desired by the Physicians.

At the time of his decease Dr. Craik and myself were in the situation before mentioned; Mrs. Washington was sitting near the foot of the bed. Christopher was standing by the bedside. Caroline Molly & Charlotte were in the room standing near the door. Mrs. Forbes the House keeper, was frequently in the room during the day and evening.

As soon as Dr. Craik could speak after the distressing scene was closed, he desired one of the servants to ask the Gentln. below to come upstairs. When they came to the bedside; I kissed the cold hand which I had held to my bosom; laid it down, & went to the other end of the room; where I was for some time lost in profound grief; until aroused by Christopher desiring me to take care of the General's keys and other things which were taken out of his pockets; and which Mrs. Washington directed him to give to me: I wrapped them in the General's handkerchief, & took them with me to my room.

About 12 o'clk the Corpse was brought down stairs, and laid out in the large room. (Note: the account continues to the closing of Washington's tomb on December 25th.)

ENDNOTES

1 George Washington [hereafter GW] to Jonathan Trumbull, 30 Aug. 1799, in W.W. Abbot et al., eds., *The Papers of George Washington:* [hereafter GWP] Retirement Series (4 vols.; Charlottesville and London,1998-99), 4:276.

2 John Adams to Abigail Adams, March 5, 1797, in *Letters of John Adams Addressed to His Wife*, (2 vols.; Boston, 1842), 2:244.

3 Thomas Fleming, "Presidents Presidents Like." Available on line at http://www.tompaine.com/history/2000/08/04/12.html.

4 GW to James Anderson, 7April 1797, in GWP *Retirement Series*, 1:79.

5 GW to Tobias Lear, 9 March 1797, in ibid., 1:25.

6 GW to William Gordon 15 Oct. 1797, in ibid., 1:407.

7 "Lady Henrietta Liston's Journal of Washington's "Resignation," Retirement, and Death," *Pennsylvania Magazine of History and Biography* 95 (1971), pp. 516-17.

8 W.W. Abbot, "George Washington in Retirement." Available on line at the George Washington Papers home page. http://www.virginia.edu/gwpapers/articles/retire/index.html.

9 GW to marquis de Lafayette, 25 Dec. 1798, in GWP *Retirement Series*, 3:281-82.

10 Abbot, "Retirement...", see note 8.

11 This point is developed in Garry Wills, *Cincinnatus: George Washington and the Enlightenment* (Garden City, N.Y., 1984).

12 Noemie Emery, *Washington: A Biography* (London, 1976), pp. 381-82.

13 Abbot, "Retirement...," see note 8.

14 William Thornton to John Lettsom, 9 Oct. 1797, in C.M Harris and Daniel Preston, eds., *Papers of William Thornton*, vol. 1: 1781-1802 (Charlottesville and London, 1995), p. 423.

15 Abbot, "Retirement...", see note 8.

16 Tobias Lear to Mary Stillson Lear, 16 Dec. 1799, copy in information file on George Washington's death, Mount Vernon Ladies' Association, Mount Vernon, Va. [hereafter MVLA].

17 I am grateful to Dr. David Morens of the National Institute of Health for sharing his knowledge of the disease epiglottitis with me. See David H. Morens, "Death of a President," *New England Journal of Medicine*, Vol. 341, No. 24 (1999), pp. 1845-1849.

18 Elisha Dick, "Facts and Observations Relative to the Disease of Cynanche Trachealis, or Croup," *Philadelphia Medical & Physical Journal*, 1809 (May, Supplement 3), pp. 242-55.

19 Thomas Law to Edward Law, first baron Ellenborough, 15 Dec. 1799, copy in file on the death of George Washington, *The Papers of George Washington* project, University of Virginia, Charlottesville [hereafter GWPP]. This interesting letter is reprinted in the 1972 Annual Report of the Mount Vernon Ladies' Association.

20 Ray Brighton, *The Checkered Career of Tobias Lear* (Portsmouth, N.H., 1985), pp.

42,44.

21   Tobias Lear to GW, 24 April 1791, GWP Presidential Series (8 vols. to date; Charlottesville and London, 1993 -), 8:131-32.

22   Brighton, *Checkered Career*, pp. 150-52. GW to Tobias Lear, 25 June 1798, in GWP Retirement Series, 2: 357.

23   Martha Washington to Unknown Recipient, 18 Sept. 1799.
      The letter is in Joseph E. Fields, ed., "Worthy Partner": *The Papers of Martha Washington*, (Westport, Conn., 1994), p. 321. Fields comments, "the letter seems consistent with the facts." [p. 322] In the author's opinion, the authenticity of this letter is highly suspect and it is not to be trusted. The reasons for this conclusion are many. The letter, written September 18, 1799, indicated the dream led Washington to write his will, but the will was completed and signed on July 9. Would Martha think the dream so important that she would write about its importance more than two months later? While possible, it is probably unlikely that Martha was in Washington's study and going over his papers closely enough to know he was working on a will. And to whom would she write such a letter? There is no name given, but there are no examples of this type of letter to other kinfolk.
      Additionally, the tone, vocabulary and spelling are not consistent with letters that Martha wrote on her own. Many of her more eloquent letters were written for her by her husband or by his secretary. It is highly unlikely that George Washington would wish to share an intimate dream like this with other people and help her write the letter. Indeed, one of the Rules of Civility that he copied as a young man and tried to follow explicitly cautioned against the practice of sharing dreams with any intimate friends. [Number 62] Washington's dream involved angels, although Washington never referred to angels in any of his correspondence and therefore probably did not believe in them. The letter has the couple "looking forward to many more years on earth" while Washington constantly emphasized his days on earth were likely to be few. The letter also paints a picture of Martha trying to coax GW into a more cheerful mood and even to her referring to the "absurdity" of his position. That does not ring true, and it would not have been typical of their relationship where Washington was, except in matters dealing with children, the dominant partner.
      The clinching argument is that Martha says Washington shared his dream with her while they were "sitting in the summer house." There was a summer house in the 19th century (!) built on the foundation of the 18th century ice house, but there was no structure called the "summer house" in the time of Washington's life and no reference to it in the 18th century literature about Mount Vernon. The reasons why the letter was forged remain a mystery, but it is another example of the need to treat cautiously such efforts to portray Washington in a more down-to-earth, folksy kind of fashion.

24   J. K. Paulding, *A Life of Washington* (2 vols.; New York, 1839), 2:196.

25   Douglas Southall Freeman et al., *George Washington: A Biography* (7 vols.; New

York, 1948-1957), 7:582-3.

26 Joseph Ellis, "The Farewell: Washington's Wisdom at the End," in Don Higginbotham, ed., *George Washington Reconsidered*, forthcoming, University of Virginia Press, 2000.

27 Martha Washington to Elizabeth Willing Powel, 18 Dec. 1797, in Fields, ed., *Worthy Partner*, p. 310.

28 I wish to credit Frank Grizzard for this quotation.

29 GW to Landon Carter, 5 Oct. 1798, in GWP Retirement Series, 3:79.

30 GW to William Pearce, Jan. 1795, in ibid., 4:506.

31 John E. Ferling, *The First of Men: A Life of George Washington* (Knoxville, 1988), p. 477.

32 See Samuel Eliot Morison, "The Young Man Washington," in James Morton Smith, ed., *George Washington: A Profile* (New York, 1969).

33 Quoted in Tom Wolfe, *A Man in Full* (New York, 1999), p. 475.

34 Morison, "Young Man Washington," p. 46.

35 GW to John Augustine Washington, 31 May 1754, in GWP *Colonial Series* (10 vols.; Charlottesville, 1983-95), 1:118. The king commented that Washington would not say so if he had heard many (ibid., 1:119 n.1).

36 GW to Robert Dinwiddie, 11 Oct. 1755, in ibid., 2:102.

37 GW, "Remarks", in ibid., 6:122.

38 GW to Robert Dinwiddie, 22 April 1756, in ibid., 3:33.

39 GW to Robert Dinwiddie, 29 May, 1754, in ibid., 1:107.

40 The description of Washington − "cool like a Bishop at his prayers"- by Roger Atkinson in 1774 seems particularly appropriate for Washington's actions under fire (quoted in Freeman, et al., Washington, 3:370 n. 148).

41 Emery, Washington, pp. 378-79.

42 GW to Sally Cary Fairfax, 12 Sept. 1758, in GWP Colonial Series, 6:42.

43 Wills, *Cincinnatus*, p. 174.

44 GW to marquis de Lafayette, 28 July 1791, in GWP Presidential Series, 8:377.

45 David Humphreys to Martha Washington, 5 July 1800, in Fields, ed., *Worthy Partner*, p. 389.

46 Quoted in George Washington Nordham, *George Washington's Religious Faith* (Chicago, 1986), pp. 28-9.

47 Martha Washington to Mercy Otis Warren, 12 June 1790, in Fields, ed., *Worthy Partner*, p. 226.

48 GW to James Craik, 8 Sept. 1789, in GWP Retirement Series, 4:1.

49 I wish to credit Richard Brookhiser for this observation.

50 Edwin S. Gaustad, *Sworn Upon the Altar of God: A Religious Biography of Thomas Jefferson* (Grand Rapids, Mich. and Cambridge, 1996), p. 143.

50A GW to Thaddeus Kosciuszko, 31 Aug. 1797, in GWP Retirement Series, 1:178, note 1 .

51 GW to David Humphreys, 23 March 1793, in John C. Fitzpatrick, ed., The Writings of George Washington from the Original Manuscript Sources, 1745-1799 (39 vols.; Washington, D.C., 1931-1944) [hereafter Fitzpatrick] 32:398.

51A GW to William A. Washington, 27 Feb. 1798, in ibid., 36:171.

52   GW to Sally Cary Fairfax, 12 Sept. 1758, in GWP Colonial Series, 6:11.

53   GW to George Augustine Washington, 27 Jan. 1793, in Fitzpatrick, 32:315-16.

54   GW to William Pearce, 25 May 1794, in ibid., 33:375.

55   GW to Bryan Fairfax, 6 March 1793, in ibid., 32:376.

56   GW to Henry Lee, 27 Aug. 1790, in GWP Presidential Series, 6:347 (first quotation); GW to Tobias Lear, 30 March 1796, in Fitzpatrick, 35:5 (second quotation).

57   GW to Henry Knox, 8 Sept. 1791, in ibid., 31:360; GW to George Lewis, 9 April 1797, in GWP Retirement Series, 1:90.

58   John Parke Custis to GW, 5 July 1773, in ibid., 9:265.

59   Ferling, First of Men, p. 306. Ferling speculates that he broke off his journal entry as "if in his pain and despair he might record unmanly thoughts." There is unfortunately no way of knowing.

60   GW to Burgess Ball, 22 Sept. 1799, in GWP Retirement Series, 4: 318; GW to Betty Lewis Washington, 13 Sept. 1789, in GWP Presidential Series, 4:32; GW to George Lewis, 9 April 1797, in GWP Retirement Series, 1:90.

61   GW to Bushrod Washington, 10 Jan. 1787, in GWP Confederation Series (6 vols.; Charlottesville and London, 1992-97), 4:509-100 (first quotation); GW to Fanny Bassett Washington, 24 Feb. 1793, in Fitzpatrick, 32:354 (second quotation); GW to Henry Lee, 20 Jan 1793, in ibid., 32:309 (third and fourth quotations).

61A GW, Biographical Memorandum (c.1786), quoted in GWP Colonial Series, 1:332-33.

62   Richard Brookhiser, Founding Father (New York, 1996), p. 144.

63   William Fairfax to Lawrence Washington, 2 Oct. 1747, in Moncure Conway, Barons of the Potomac and the Rappahannock (New York, 1892), p. 256. George Mason to Sarah Mason McCarty, 10 Feb. 1785, in Robert A. Rutland, ed., The Papers of George Mason, 1725-1792 (3 vols.; Chapel Hill, 1970), 2:810.

64   Quoted in Gaustad, Sworn on the Altar of God, p. 142.

65   Paul Boller, George Washington & Religion (Dallas, 1963), p. 114.

65A GW to David Humphreys, 10 Oct. 1787 in GWP Confederation Series, vol. 5:365.

66   GW to Henry Knox, 27 April 1787, in GWP Confederation Series, 5:157; GW to Betty Washington Lewis, 13 Sept. 1789, in GWP Presidential Series, 4:32; GW to marquis de Lafayette, 8 Dec. 1784, in GWP Confederation Series, 2:175.

67   John Parke Custis to Martha Washington, 5 July 1773, in Fields, ed., Worthy Partner, pp. 152-53; John Parke Custis to GW, 5 July 1773, in GWP Colonial Series, 9:265.

68   For readers wishing the citations for these quotes, see Peter Henriques, "The Final Struggle Between George Washington and the Grim King: Washington's Attitude Toward Death and Afterlife," Virginia Magazine of History and Biography, vol. 107, no. 1 (1999), notes 57 & 58, pp. 94-95. See also GW to

Tobias Lear, 30 March 1796, in *Fitzpatrick*, 35:5-6; Charles Callahan, *Washington: The Man and the Mason* (Washington, D.C., 1913), pp. 274 & 276.

69 GW to Robert Stewart, 10 Aug. 1783, in *Fitzpatrick*, 27:88.

70 GW to Burwell Bassett, 20 June 1773, in GWP Colonial Series, 9:243 (quotation); Burgess Ball to GW, 25 Aug. 1789, in GWP Presidential Series, 3:356; GW to Betty Washington Lewis, 13 Sept. 1789, in ibid., 4:32.

71 GW to Richard Washington, 20 Oct. 1761, in GWP Colonial Series, 7:80.

72 GW to George William Fairfax, 11 March 1778, in *Fitzpatrick*, 11:62-3.

73 GW to Alexander Hamilton, 27 May 1798, in GWP Retirement Series, 2:298.

74 See for example, GW to marquis de Lafayette, 8 Dec. 1784, in *Fitzpatrick*, 28:6-7; GW to James Craik, 8 Sept. 1789, in GWP Presidential Series, 4:1.

75 Barry Schwartz, *George Washington: The Making of an American Symbol*, (New York and London, 1987), p. 175.

76 GW's *Circular to the States*, 8 June 1783, in Fitzpatrick,, 26:496.

77 GW to marquis de Lafayette, 15 Aug. 1787, in *Fitzpatrick*, 29:259; Freeman, et al., Washington, 2:387-88, 397.

78 I wish to give credit to Dr. Phil Chase for this observation.

79 GW to Henry Lee, 22 Sept. 1788, in GWP Confederation Series, 6:530.

80 Carl J. Richard, *The Founders and the Classics* (Cambridge, Mass. and London, 1994), p. 185.

81 Freeman et al., *Washington*, 5: 500.

82 GW to marquis de Lafayette, 28 May 1788, in GWP Confederation Series, 6:297; David Humphreys to GW, 17 July 1787, in ibid., 3:131.

83 GW to James Tilghman, 5 June 1786, in ibid., 4:96.

84 Fisher Ames, *An Oration on the Sublime Virtues of General George Washington*, p. 48. Copy at MVLA.

85 GW to Burgess Ball, 22 Sept. 1799, in GWP Retirement Series, 4:318.

85A Henriettea Liston, *Journal*, p. 519.

86 C. M. Harris and Daniel Preston, eds., *Papers of William Thornton*, vol. 1:1781-1802 (Charlottesville and London, 1995), p. 423.

87 John Enys Journal, 1788, in "Descriptions of Martha Washington," Loose-leaf notebook, MVLA.

88 Thomas Lee Shippen, 1790, in ibid.

89 Gouverneur Morris, *An Oration upon the Death of General Washington*, 31 Dec. 1799 (New York, 1800), p.8., Copy at MVLA.

90 Charles Pinckney Sumner, "Eulogy on the Illustrious Life of George Washington", in *Eulogies & Orations* (Boston, 1800), p. 269. Copy at MVLA.

91 Rudolf Marx, "A Medical Profile of George Washington," *American Heritage* (1955, No. 6), p. 106.

92 Dr. Craik said it was around 11 a.m. The account of Drs. Craik and Dick was published in the *Times and Alexandria Advertiser*, 19 Dec. 1799; copy on file at GWPP and MVLA.

93 The appraisers in 1800 valued the "Tambur Secretary" at $80 and the "Circular chair" at $20. GWP Retirement Series, 4:503. Fortunately, these "priceless

items" are now safely back in Washington's study. Washington also gave Craik his fishing tackle box and that too has been preserved.

94 James Craik to GW, 31 Aug. 1791 , in GWP Presidential Series, 8:473.

95 GW to James Craik, 26 April 1777, in GWP Revolutionary War Series (10 vols. to date; Charlottesville and London, 1985 -), 9:273.

96 Editors' note, ibid.

97 GW to James McHenry, 3 July 1789, in *Fitzpatrick*, 30:351.

98 GW to James Craik, 8 Sept. 1789, in GWP Presidential Series, 4:1.

99 GW to James McHenry, 5 July 1798, in GWP Retirement Series, 2:384.

100 Tobias Lear to Gustavus Brown 14 Dec. 1799, copy at MVLA.

101 The three best studies are White McKenzie Wallenborn, "George Washington's Terminal Illness," copy in file at GWPP; Heinz H. E. Scheidemandel, MD, "Did George Washington Die of Quinsy?", *Arch Otolaryngol*, vol. 102, September, 1976. Copy in information file on Washington's death, MVLA; David Morens, "Death of a President," *New England Journal of Medicine*, vol. 341, No. 24, December, 1999. Drooling was not explicitly mentioned but had to have occurred since GW was unable to swallow his saliva and mucous. It is perhaps noteworthy that Dr. Dick performed an autopsy on one young patient and recorded, "The first thing that arrested my attention, was the great difficulty and almost impracticality of passing a common probe through the glottis. It exhibited a degree of tumefaction, but more manifestly a rigid stricture. On preceding downwards, no remnant of membranous concretion appeared in the slight appearances of inflammation." Dick, "Facts and Observations," Philadelphia Medical Journal, p. 247. The phrase "epiglottitis" was first used in 1830.

102 Levin Powell to Col. Charles Simms, 18 Dec. 1799, in *George Washington: Condolences & Funeral Transcriptions*, vol. 1, MVLA.

103 Mason Locke Weems, *The Life of George Washington*, Peter Onuf, ed. (Armonk, N.Y. and London, 1996), p. 133.

103A *Alexandria Gazette*, December, 1931, Vol. 2, No. 3. Copy in box on George Washington's Death, MVLA.

104 George Washington Nordham, "200 Years at Rest: Revisiting the Death of George Washington," GW Magazine, (George Washington University), Fall, 1999, p. 19.

105 Bryan Fairfax to Earl of Buchan, 28 Jan. 1800, copy in box of material dealing with GW's death and funeral, MVLA.

106 Quoted in Willard Sterne Randall, *George Washington: A Life* (New York, 1997), p. 44.

107 Gustavus Brown to James Craik, quoted in Freeman, et. al., *Washington*, 7:643.

108 Marx, "Medical Profile", p. 44.

109 Peter Stavrakis, "Heroic medicine, bloodletting, and the sad fate of George Washington," *Maryland Medical Journal*, vol. 46, no. 10 (Nov./Dec., 1997), p. 539.

110 Richard Norton Smith, *Patriarch*, (Boston and New York, 1993), p. 353.

111 Benjamin Rush, perhaps on information received from Dr. Dick, asserted the General's chief concern during the ordeal had not been survival, but rather that his physicians "enable him to die easy."

112 Tobias Lear to Alexander Hamilton, 16 Jan. 1800, in Harold C Syrett, ed., *The Papers of Alexander Hamilton* vol. 24(New York, 1976), p. 199.

113 Quoted in Smith, *Patriarch*, p. 359.

114 Abigail Adams to sister, 22 Dec. 1799, copy in file on the death of George Washington, MVLA.

115 William Thornton, "On National Education", note 32 in Harris., ed., Thornton Papers, 1:366.

116 Smith, Patriarch, p. 304.

117 W.S. Baker, *Character Sketches of George Washington* (Philadelphia, 1887), pp. 175-76.

118 Wyndham Blanton, *Annals of Medical History*, vol. 5 (1933), p. 54. Copy at the GWPP.

119 GW to William Soy, 14 Oct. 1797, in GWP Retirement Series, I:404; GW to George Washington Lafayette, 5 Dec. 1797, in ibid., 1:506.

120 GW to Roger West, 19 Sept. 1799, in GWP Retirement Series, 4:310.

121 GW to George Steptoe Washington, 5 Dec. 1790, in *Fitzpatrick*, 31:162-63 (first quotation); GW to James Anderson, 21 Dec. 1797, in *Fitzpatrick*, 36:113 (second quotation); GW to James Anderson, 13 Dec. 1799, in GWP Retirement Series, 4:467 (third quotation).

122 Editorial Note, ibid., 4:478.

123 Freeman, et al., *Washington*, 7:583-84.

124 GW to Tobias Lear, 2 Aug. 1798, in GWP Retirement Series, 2:483 (first quotation); quoted in Freeman et al., *Washington*, 7:583 (second quotation).

125 W.W. Abbot, "An Uncommon Awareness of Self: The Papers of George Washington," Prologue 21 (1989), p. 7.

126 GW to Lund Washington, 17 Dec. 1776, in *Fitzpatrick*, 37: 536; editorial note, GWP Retirement Series 4:500; Abbot, "An Uncommon Awareness," p. 15.

127 David Humphreys to GW, 17 July 1785, in GWP Confederation Series, 3:131.

128 Freeman et al., *Washington*, 7:624; Sumner, *Eulogies*, p. 269. Copy at MVLA.

129 Bryan Fairfax to Earl of Buchan, 28 Jan. 1800, copy in box of material dealing with GW's death and funeral, MVLA; Tobias Lear to William A. Washington, 15 Dec. 1799, in Worthington Chauncey Ford, ed., *The Writings of Washington* (14 vols.; New York and London, 1889-93), 14:257.

130 Patrick Henry to Anne Henry Christian, 15 May 1786, in William Wirt Henry, *Patrick Henry* (3 vols., 1891; New York, 1969), 2:286-87 (first quotation); Patrick Henry to Bartholomew Dandridge, 21 Jan. 1785, in ibid., 2:252 (second quotation); Dorothy Dandridge Henry to Elizabeth Henry Aylett, n.d., Patrick Henry Memorial Association, Brookneal, Va. (third quotation).

131 Thomas Law to Edward Law, first baron Ellenborough, 18 Dec. 1799, copy in file on the death of George Washington, GWPP.

132 Boller, *Washington and Religion*, p. 89.

133 GW to Bryan Fairfax, 20 Jan. 1799, in GWP Retirement Series, 3:325.

134 GW to Robert Dinwiddie, 29 May 1754, in GWP Colonial Series, 1:107.

135 John Marshall, *Life of George Washington* (5 vols.; 1804; New York, 1925) 5:362. According to Worthington Ford, this assertion was based on a private letter from Dr. Craik to John Marshall; Ford, ed., *The Writings of Washington*, 14:256.

136 Freeman, et al., *Washington*, 7:603-4; Wyndham Blanton, *18th Century Medicine in Virginia*, (Richmond, 1931), p. 304.

137 Dick, "Facts and Observations," *Philadelphia Medical Journal*, p. 253. [See also Elisha Dick to Thomas Semmes, 10 January 1800, in, J.A. Nydeggar, "The last illness of George Washington," Medical Record, vol. 92 (1917), p. 1128.]

138 Ibid., p.246.

139 Ibid., p.253.

140 In Lear's later "diary" account he says "three days" which was more customary. Washington most likely said "two days" for that is what Lear wrote the day following his death and repeated to his mother on the 16th. Additionally, Thomas Law, writing on the day after GW's death, uses "two days" as well, obviously repeating what Lear told him.

141 Hannah Washington, *Will and Final testament*, 17 June 1800. Copy at MVLA.

142 I wish to credit Mary Thompson of MVLA for this information.

143 GW to Nathaniel Gorman, 21 July 1788, in GWP Confederation Series, 6:372-73 and n. 1.

144 There is debate, depending on how the accounts are read, as to whether GW closed his eyes on his own or whether Dr. Craik did so. Quotation is from William Martin, *Citizen Washington*, (New York, 1999), p. 574.

145 Tobias Lear to Mary Stillson Lear, 16 Dec. 1799, in information file on George Washington's death, MVLA. This letter refers to Martha's comment about "rejoicing" to follow GW to the grave, although this is not in Lear's longer "diary" account.

146 Tobias Lear to George Washington Parke Custis and Lawrence Lewis, 15 Dec. 1799, in *George Washington: Condolences & Funeral Transcriptions*, vol. 1, MVLA.

147 William Thornton, draft appended to essay, "On Sleep", in Harris., ed., Thornton Papers, 1:528.

148 Catherine Albanese, "Newness Transcending: Civil Religion and the American Revolution," *Southern Quarterly*, vol. 14, no. 4 (1974), p. 322. Claude C. Robin, 1781, in Baker, ed., *Character Sketches*, p.17.

149 Paul K. Longmore, *The Invention of George Washington* (Berkeley, Los Angeles and London, 1988), pp. 1 & 211.

150 I wish to credit Richard Brookhiser for this observation.

151 One provocative new study goes so far as to argue, on compelling, but not completely convincing, circumstantial evidence, that Washington, for reasons of statecraft to strengthen the union, actually desired and indeed orchestrated a plan to have his body entombed in a special mausoleum in the very center of the United States Capitol building designed by his good friend, Dr. William Thornton. One strong point against that argument is that GW in his will

explicitly ordered a new larger burial vault be built at Mount Vernon and that his remains be interred there. Was this request all part of an intricate ruse? Did he in confidence tell intimates like Lear or his wife that he actually wished to be buried at the Capitol? There is no concrete evidence that he did. C.M. Harris, "Washington's Gamble, L'Enfant's Dream: Politics, Design, and the Founding of the National Capital," *William and Mary Quarterly,* 3rd Series, vol. 56, no. 3, (July, 1999), pp. 559-64.

152 Thomas Law to Edward Law, first baron Ellenborough, 18 Dec. 1799, copy in file on the death of George Washington, GWPP.

153 The various bills discussed are located either the box of material dealing with GW's death and funeral or in the binder, *George Washington: Condolences & Funeral Transcriptions,* vol. 1. Both are at MVLA.

154 Virginia Herald, 31 Dec. 1799, Copy in box of material dealing with GW's death and funeral, MVLA. Last sentence quoted from F. L. Brockett, *The Lodge of Washington,* (Alexandria, 1876), p. 100.

155 Callahan, Washington: *The Man and the Mason,* p. 302.

156 Thomas Law to Edward Law, first baron Ellenborough, 18 Dec. 1799, copy in file on the death of George Washington, GWPP. The quote about the slaves mourning is in no author, *Washingtoniana,* (Privately reprinted, New York, 1865), p. 179.

157 Benjamin Rush, *Commonplace Book,* 14 Dec. 1799, in George Corner, ed., *Benjamin Rush Autobiography* (Westport, Conn., 1970), p .249. Partisanship did not play much a role in the immediate period of mourning, although the Republicans were concerned about the political benefits that the Federalists might accrue from GW's death. Later, John Adams wrote about to this to Thomas Jefferson. "The Death of W. diffused a general grief. The Old tories, the Hyperfederalists, the Speculators, set up a general Howl. Orations Prayers Sermons Mock Funerals were all employed, not that they loved Washington but to keep in countenance the Funding and Banking system." John Adams to Thomas Jefferson, 3 Sept. 1816, in Lester Cappon, ed., Adams - *Jefferson Letters* (2 vols.; Chapel Hill, 1988) 2:488.

158 Fisher Ames, *Oration,* p. 7.

159 S. Crawford to his mother, 24 Dec. 1799, copy in *George Washington: Condolence Book,* vol. 1, MVLA.

160 "Funeral Procession in Baltimore", Washingtoniana, p. 240.

161 Ibid.

162 *Virginia Gazette,* 20 Dec. 1799, copy in box of material dealing with GW's death and funeral, MVLA.

163 Thomas Law to Edward Law, first baron Ellenborough, 18 Dec. 1799, copy in file on the death of George Washington, GWPP.

164 Alexander Hamilton in Syrett, ed., *Hamilton Papers,* 24:112.

165 This paragraph in a close paraphrase of Emery, Washington, p. 375-76 and the *Pennsylvania Gazette,* 1 Jan. 1800.

166 J. Russell's *Gazette* (Boston), 2 Jan. 1800. Original copy in the Special

Collections, University of Virginia Alderman Library.

167   Schwartz, *American Symbol*, p. 93.

168   Catherine Albanese, "Newness Transcending: Civil Religion and the
       American Revolution," *Southern Quarterly*, vol. 14, no. 4 (1974), p. 323; Barry
       Schwartz, "The Character of Washington: A Study in American Culture,"
       American Quarterly, vol. 38, no. 2 (1986), p. 202; Harris, ed. Thornton Papers,
       1:537.

169   Robert Hay, "George Washington: American Moses," *American Quarterly*, vol.
       21, no. 4 (1969), pp. 781 & 788.

170   Alexander Hamilton to Tobias Lear, 2 Jan. 1800, in Syrett, ed., *Hamilton
       Papers*, 24:155.

171   Brookhiser, *Founding Father*, p. 199.

172   Emery, *Washington*, p. 369.

173   Earl of Buchan to Martha Washington, 28 Jan. 1800, in Fields, ed., *Worthy
       Partner*, p. 346.

174   Thomas Law to Edward Law, first baron Ellenborough, 18 Dec. 1799, copy in
       file on the death of George Washington, GWPP; S. Lyman to his wife, Mary,
       7 Jan. 1800, in George Washington Condolence Book, vol. 1, MVLA.

175   Morris, *An Oration*, pp. 23-24.

176   Tobias Lear to William Prescott, 4 March 1788, quoted in John Knowlton,
       "Tobias Lear and George Washington: In Support of Greatness" (M.A.
       Thesis, University of Maine, 1967), p. 4. Copy at MVLA.

177   Brighton, *Checkered Career*, p. 116.

178   The account of Drs. Craik and Dick was published in the *Times and
       Alexandria Advertiser*, 19 Dec. 1799, copy on file at GWPP and MVLA.

179   Thomas Law to Edward Law, first baron Ellenborough, 18 Dec. 1799, copy in
       file on the death of George Washington, GWPP.

180   For discussion of the two editions, see editorial note, GWP Retirement
       Series, 4:552-55.

181   Weems, *The Life of Washington*, p. 134.

182   I wish to thank Dr. Ken Wallenborn for this information.

ABOUT THE AUTHOR

Peter R. Henriques is an Associate Professor of History at George Mason University. He teaches American and Virginia history with special emphasis on Virginia, and the American Revolution and the Virginia Founding Fathers. Recently, he was appointed by Mount Vernon to the Advisory Council of George Washington Scholars.

The editor of the local history journal, *Northern Virginia Heritage,* his writings include: "The Final Struggle Between George Washington and the Grim King: Washington's Attitude Toward Death and Afterlife," *Virginia Magazine of History and Biography,* winter 1999; "Major Lawrence Washington Versus the Reverend Charles Green: A Case Study of the Squire and the Parson," *VMHB,* April 1992; "An Uneven Friendship: The Relationship Between George Washington and George Mason," *VMHB,* April 1989. He was a participant in, and the historical consultant for, the video biography of George Washington released by A&E in 2000. Currently, he is working on a brief biography of George Washington for the National Park Service and on a study examining the subject of George Washington and religion.

He lives with his wife, Marlene, in Fairfax County, Virginia, and is the father of four grown sons—Mark, Thomas, Gregg, and Timothy.

LIST OF ILLUSTRATIONS

Cover   *George Washington in his Last Illness*
Etching by unidentified artist
Donated to Mount Vernon by Mrs. Wilmarth Sheldon Lewis

iv   Bust of George Washington, 1785
By Jean Antoine Houdon

7   Tobias Lear, anonymous
Courtesy Portsmouth Marine Society

23   *The Apotheosis of George Washington*
by David Edwin after Rembrandt Peale, 1800

34   Bleeding instruments on George Washington's bedside table.
Photograph by Robert Lautman

51   *The Death of Washington*
Sketch in Oil by Howard Pyle, 1896
Courtesy Boston Public Library

58   The Old Tomb at Mount Vernon
Photograph by Robert Lautman

63   Miniature Portrait of George Washington
Watercolor on paper by Madame la Marquise de Brehan, 1788